T0284760

THE CHANGING CHRISTIAN WORLD

A Brief Introduction for JEWS

RABBI LEONARD A. SCHOOLMAN

For People of All Faiths, All Backgrounds
JEWISH LIGHTS Publishing
Woodstock, Vermont

The Changing Christian World:
A Brief Introduction for Jews

2008 First Printing
© 2008 by Leonard A. Schoolman

For information regarding permission to reprint material from this book, please write or fax your request to Jewish Lights Publishing, Permissions Department, at the address / fax number listed below, or e-mail your request to permissions@jewishlights.com.

Library of Congress Cataloging-in-Publication Data
Schoolman, Leonard A.
   The changing Christian world : a brief introduction for Jews / by Rabbi Leonard A. Schoolman.
      p. cm.
   Includes bibliographical references.
   ISBN-13: 978-1-58023-344-6 (quality pbk.)
   ISBN-10: 1-58023-344-9 (quality pbk.)
   1. Christianity—21st century. 2. Christianity and other religions—Judaism. 3. Judaism—Relations—Christianity. I. Title.
   BR121.3.S36 2008
   270.02'4296—dc22

                                                                    2008000612

10   9   8   7   6   5   4   3   2   1

Manufactured in the United States of America
Cover Design: Melanie Robinson

For People of All Faiths, All Backgrounds
Published by Jewish Lights Publishing
A Division of LongHill Partners, Inc.
Sunset Farm Offices, Route 4, P.O. Box 237
Woodstock, VT 05091
Tel: (802) 457-4000   Fax: (802) 457-4004
www.jewishlights.com

For
DIANA
with whom all things are possible

CONTENTS

ACKNOWLEDGMENTS

I AM DEEPLY GRATEFUL TO EMILY WICHLAND, vice president of editorial and production at Jewish Lights, and her gracious and friendly staff, particularly project editor Mark Ogilbee, for all their support.

Walter Taylor and Bill Tully, both friends now for many years, have been enthusiastic supporters of the Center for Religious Inquiry (CRI) at St. Bartholomew's Church in New York and the then Center for Theological Studies at Christ Church Cathedral in Houston.

Many lay leaders at St. Bart's have given enthusiastic support over the years. Richard Bayles, the current chair of CRI, has been one of our chief cheerleaders at every juncture and even a chauffeur, shlepping me to Yale Divinity School on almost my first day on the job. Kate Briggs (and her husband, John), now a warden at St. Bart's and a former chair, and Robert Gutheil, the first chair, and Senator George Mitchell, a former chair, all "got it." Dr. Robert Radtke, CRI vice chair, gave freely of his counsel, and took me to his alma mater, Columbia University, to introduce me to members of the faculty. All of these lay leaders were always there to do what needed to be done to make CRI a success.

My children, Dr. Martha E. Schoolman and Abigail Schoolman-Stevens have always stimulated me to learn more

ACKNOWLEDGMENTS

and to do more. Their spouses, Caitlin and Wade, and baby Lila ask good questions. That too is indeed a gift.

Friends, including Rabbi Daniel Polish, the Reverend Arthur Kennedy, the Reverend Dennis McManus, and Rabbi Leon Klenicki, all made contributions to this book in many ways, visible and invisible. The Reverend Mark Bozzuti-Jones, a former Jesuit who is now an Episcopal priest, read sections of an earlier version of this book, and he made many excellent suggestions. My editor Arthur Goldwag made a number of helpful suggestions. The responsibility for the final work, of course, is all mine.

Finally, the overworked staff at St. Bart's always managed to help us get done what needed to be done. Thank you.

viii

HOW THE CHRISTIAN WORLD HAS CHANGED

THIS BOOK COULD NOT HAVE BEEN WRITTEN fifty years ago. In fact, it would have been beyond the capacities of even the most prescient among us to imagine the changes that have so transformed the religious community in America and the world.

The 1960s have been widely derided as an era of untrammeled self-expression. The symbol of the era was Woodstock, which took place in 1969, but the whole decade was marked by widespread manifestations of the American "counterculture"—flower children, drugs, hippies, and rampant idealism. But it was also in the 1960s that a very important, frequently overlooked, series of events changed the face of Jewish America.

The stage had been set in the years after World War II. While it is true that some Jews had played a significant economic role in America before the war, we did not like to advertise our prominence in the financial world. We did not want to push our way forward. We preferred to remain in the safety of our own communities, whether we were German immigrants from the nineteenth century or Eastern European Jews who came at the beginning of the twentieth century. We seemed content in our neighborhoods, clubs, synagogues, and traditional enclaves.

World War II changed all that. Young Jewish boys who had grown up in the ghettos of the Northeast and the

Midwest spent weeks and months sharing foxholes in Europe and the Far East with people whom they had never before met—Catholics and Protestants. The G.I. Bill of Rights, which enabled veterans to attend college at the expense of the United States government, created a new class of educated Jewish professionals in the 1950s. Freshly minted Jewish lawyers, doctors, and accountants began to move to the new suburbs that were springing up everywhere. They created and joined new Reform and Conservative synagogues, just as their Christian neighbors built new churches. Jewish theologian and sociologist Will Herberg wrote his famous sociological study *Protestant, Catholic, Jew* about this new phenomenon in 1955. His book explained how the role of immigrants had changed. They had become the real Americans, and with their varying religious traditions they were changing the face of our country. The United States was no longer the exclusive control of the Protestant majority.

Jews were no longer seen as immigrants, people foreign to America, and they began to participate more actively and visibly in the life of the American community. They were Americans; they had fought for their country in numbers greater than their proportion of the population and helped win the war.

A second massive transformation began with the rise of a new concern in America for the rights of all people, especially African Americans. Civil rights leaders like the Reverend Martin Luther King, Jr., and Ralph Abernathy had dozens of rabbis and other Jews at their sides, frequently to the ire of Southern Jews. Jewish leaders such as Rabbi Abraham Joshua Heschel, Rabbi Maurice Eisendrath, president of the Union of American Hebrew Congregations (now the Union for Reform Judaism), and Albert Vorspan shared a vision of what a new and different America could be like.

It was also in the 1960s that Pope John XXIII convened the Second Vatican Council. This meeting of bishops from all over the Catholic world marked a sea change for the entire Roman Catholic Church. What resulted was a landmark declaration, known as *Nostra Aetate* ("In Our Time" in Latin; see Appendix 2), calling for respect among all religions. While many of the changes it introduced to the Church have yet to be totally absorbed, the Church's adoption of *Nostra Aetate* opened a new chapter in Jewish-Christian relations.

The document enunciated the principle that the Jewish covenant with God was still valid and had not been superseded by the New Covenant. The centuries-old denigration of Jews and contempt for Judaism as a fossil religion, important only as the precursor of Christianity, ceased; Jews became honored older brothers and sisters.

Jews were no longer viewed merely as candidates for conversion. The significance of this change in the Church cannot be overstated. *Nostra Aetate* literally changed everything, and not just for Catholics. Almost every Protestant denomination followed suit.

As these changes were occurring, a small group in the Jewish community began to reach out to the Roman Catholic Church and the various Protestant denominations. The lay and professional leadership of the American Jewish Committee (Rabbi Mark Tannenbaum and later Rabbi James Rudin) and the Anti-Defamation League (in particular Rabbi Leon Klenicki) understood how to build interfaith relationships through quiet dialogue. Christians and Jews began to get to know and trust each other.

An example of this trust is the honor paid to Rabbi Klenicki when Pope Benedict XVI named him a knight of St. Gregory in 2007. This unusual tribute was paid in

3

appreciation of the considerable work he had done to promote Catholic-Jewish dialogue.

On the Catholic side, leaders such as Sister Rose Thering, Father Edward Flannery, Father John Palikowski, Dr. Eugene Fisher, and Dr. Philip Cunningham wrote recommended guidelines for Catholic textbooks to reflect new attitudes and understandings. We are still building on the work done by these significant religious leaders and are indebted to them for their foresight and courage.

How It All Began

I have been a rabbi for over forty years. I served for eighteen years as director of programs for the Union of American Hebrew Congregations (now the Union for Reform Judaism) and for over ten years as a spiritual leader in congregations in different parts of the United States. But it is only in these last dozen years that I have devoted myself totally to interfaith work with the Christian community. In 1995, I had taken early retirement and was living in Houston. I encountered my friend the Very Reverend Walter H. Taylor, dean of Houston Christ Church Cathedral, at a meeting one day, and he asked me to serve on a committee that he was establishing. His aim was to devise a completely new program of adult education, not the usual fare that synagogues and churches offered. It was probably the best committee in which I ever had the honor of participating. We worked diligently for six months and sent our report to the dean. He was so pleased he called me and asked whether I would come downtown to direct the program. I was happy to end my retirement to do this innovative and exciting work.

The key to the program was its inter-religious character. For example, I taught a course on the book of Job, utilizing the biblical text and Rabbi Harold Kushner's book *When Bad Things Happen to Good People*. The twenty-five students were a cross section of the Christian and Jewish communities in Houston. What was remarkable was the unanimity of understanding that emerged from the group, especially when they considered their own finitude. We had created a place where Jews and Christians could learn together in a comfortable and safe environment.

Walter was delighted to tell anyone who would listen about "his rabbi." He had one of those conversations with his friend Rev. William McD. Tully, the rector of St. Bartholomew's Church in New York. Rev. Tully told Walter that he would be interested in meeting me the next time I came to New York, which turned out to be in June, 1998.

I had expected to pay a twenty-minute courtesy call on Walter's friend. Instead, my visit lasted more than two hours. By the time I returned to Houston, Bill had already sent an e-mail inviting me to return to New York the following week to meet some of the lay leaders of St. Bart's. Bill then asked me to become a consultant to help him develop a similar interfaith program. I served in that capacity until April 1999, when Walter Taylor's retirement from Christ Church Cathedral allowed Bill to invite me to come to New York and work full time at St. Bart's. We launched the Center for Religious Inquiry in the fall of 1999. Since then, we have offered almost two hundred courses to many thousands of Jews, Christians, Muslims, and other seekers of no religious affiliation, taught by senior faculty of the major universities and seminaries in the Greater New York area and beyond.

These dozen years have given me the opportunity to teach Judaism (in Introduction to Judaism classes, Bible classes, and Hebrew) to hundreds of Houstonites and New Yorkers. During my many interactions with my students I learned how little Christians know about Judaism. I also learned how little Jews know about their neighbors' religions.

So when Stuart M. Matlins, the founder and publisher of Jewish Lights, invited me to write a book for Jews about the changing Christian world, I saw it as a unique opportunity to crystallize all that I have been doing and thinking about since I began my interfaith work.

WHAT IS IN THIS BOOK?

This book is divided into two unequal parts. Since Jews know as little about Christian theology as many Christians know about Judaism, I decided to first set forth some basic principles of Christian religious thinking and compare them to Jewish teachings on the same subjects.

I believe that one of the essential differences between Judaism and Christianity is their widely divergent views about the human condition. As a result of St. Augustine's teaching about "original sin," Christian thought has developed a strongly skeptical view of human nature as profoundly affected by its own sinfulness. While it is true that not every Christian through the ages, or even today, accepts this notion, original sin is such a pervasive idea in Christian thought that to omit dealing with it up front would be a serious misjudgment.

From there, I proceed to discuss Jesus and the matter of end-times theology. There are many different visions of Jesus and his life. I try to make sense of them for a Jewish audience. End times, or what happens both at the end of the world and when we die, are peculiarly Christian preoccupations that barely enter Jewish thought. But if you have heard of the multi-million-copy selling *Left Behind* books by Tim LaHaye and Jerry B. Jenkins, I'm sure your curiosity has been kindled on such matters.

The second part of the book deals with essential issues that Jews need to know about, such as conversion efforts aimed at Jews, whether we are waiting for the Messiah, the inerrancy or literal truth of the Bible, Israel and Christian Zionism, and the political efforts of the radical right in the United States today.

I also attempt to explain two countervailing phenomena in American Christianity today: the rise of megachurches and the emergent church movement, both of which are responses to large cultural changes of our time.

In every chapter, I have included quotes from other authors whose comments might augment my argument or present a completely different point of view. I also want to emphasize that this book in no way claims to be an exhaustive exploration of Christian beliefs. My goal has been to give an entrée into the complex world of Christian belief and practice, but as in any overview, I have at times had to paint with a very broad brush. For example, what is sometimes called the "religious right"—which often refers to evangelical and fundamentalist Christians—seems to get the most media coverage these days, yet Christians of this persuasion are but a part of the expansive Christian landscape in this country, which includes probably an equal number of more moderate and liberal Christians. But because the uninitiated are perhaps most likely to have gleaned "what Christians believe" from these conservative sources, I spend a disproportionate amount of time discussing their positions on certain topics. But this is not meant to imply that all, or even most, Christians believe likewise. Furthermore, even though I discuss the official positions of some denominations on certain topics, there are frequently disagreements (sometimes quite lively) over these positions within the denomination, and even within local churches.

I have prepared a glossary of Christian terms that will probably be unfamiliar to the average Jewish reader. I have purposely limited the list to those expressions that relate to the concepts and issues under discussion in this volume. Obviously there are many technical and specialized terms that I did not include.

Finally, I have prepared a short list—Suggestions for Further Reading—of contemporary books that explore more deeply areas that I was only able to touch upon briefly and that you might find especially useful and informative. I have also included a more thorough bibliography of the books cited in this work.

For quotes from both the Hebrew Bible (roughly equivalent to what Christians call the "Old Testament") and the New Testament, I have used the New Revised Standard Version (NRSV).

All in all, I hope that Jews reading this book will get a better understanding of the changing Christian world and what they can expect to see in the next few years. Predictions are hard to make, but hopefully this book will help Jews make sense of things that sometimes seem to make no sense—at least to Jews.

1

A Jew Looks at Theology

THIS BOOK IS NOT ABOUT CHRISTIAN THEOLOGY. It is rather a guide to help Jews understand and navigate the changing Christian world in America today. I want to help you develop an appreciation for the changes, particularly in relation to Judaism and the Jewish people, that have taken place in the Christian world in the second half of the twentieth century. I will also try to anticipate the directions in which contemporary American Christianity seems to be heading.

Most Christians, like most Jews, are not theologians. Most of what they believe comes from childhood experiences, what their parents taught them, and customary belief. Christianity, like Judaism and all other religions, is a way of imposing some order out of the chaos of the world in which we live. Some of these attempts, while appropriate at one time or another long ago, frequently seem out of place today. Religious traditions are often reluctant to surrender ancient beliefs that were comforting, if not correct.

The Bible gives us two accounts of Creation. Both are extraordinarily beautiful ways of looking at the origin of the world. The first version includes all of Genesis chapter 1 and the first verses of chapter 2. The focus of this first story of Creation seems to be to respond to the question "How did we get here?"

[1]In the beginning when God created the heavens and the earth, [2]the earth was a formless void and darkness covered the face of the deep, while a wind from God swept over the face of the waters. [3]Then God said, "Let there be light"; and there was light. [4]And God saw that the light was good; and God separated the light from the darkness. [5]God called the light Day, and the darkness he called Night. And there was evening and there was morning, the first day.

[6]And God said, "Let there be a dome in the midst of the waters, and let it separate the waters from the waters." [7]So God made the dome and separated the waters that were under the dome from the waters that were above the dome. And it was so. [8]God called the dome Sky. And there was evening and there was morning, the second day.

[9]And God said, "Let the waters under the sky be gathered together into one place, and let the dry land appear." And it was so. [10]God called the dry land Earth, and the waters that were gathered together he called Seas. And God saw that it was good. [11]Then God said, "Let the earth put forth vegetation: plants yielding seed, and fruit trees of every kind on earth that bear fruit with the seed in it." And it was so. [12]The earth brought forth vegetation: plants yielding seed of every kind, and trees of every kind bearing fruit with the seed in it. And God saw that it was good. [13]And there was evening and there was morning, the third day.

[14]And God said, "Let there be lights in the dome of the sky to separate the day from the night; and let them be for signs and for seasons and for days and years, [15]and let them be lights in the dome of the sky to give light upon the earth." And it was so. [16]God made the two great lights—the greater light to rule the day and the lesser light

to rule the night—and the stars. [17]God set them in the dome of the sky to give light upon the earth, [18]to rule over the day and over the night, and to separate the light from the darkness. And God saw that it was good. [19]And there was evening and there was morning, the fourth day.

[20]And God said, "Let the waters bring forth swarms of living creatures, and let birds fly above the earth across the dome of the sky." [21]So God created the great sea monsters and every living creature that moves, of every kind, with which the waters swarm, and every winged bird of every kind. And God saw that it was good. [22]God blessed them, saying, "Be fruitful and multiply and fill the waters in the seas, and let birds multiply on the earth." [23]And there was evening and there was morning, the fifth day.

[24]And God said, "Let the earth bring forth living creatures of every kind: cattle and creeping things and wild animals of the earth of every kind." And it was so. [25]God made the wild animals of the earth of every kind, and the cattle of every kind, and everything that creeps upon the ground of every kind. And God saw that it was good.

[26]Then God said, "Let us make humankind in our image, according to our likeness; and let them have dominion over the fish of the sea, and over the birds of the air, and over the cattle, and over all the wild animals of the earth, and over every creeping thing that creeps upon the earth." [27]So God created humankind in his image, in the image of God he created them; male and female he created them. [28]God blessed them, and God said to them, "Be fruitful and multiply, and fill the earth and subdue it; and have dominion over the fish of the sea and over the birds of the air and over every living thing that moves upon the earth." [29]God said, "See, I have given you every plant

yielding seed that is upon the face of all the earth, and every tree with seed in its fruit; you shall have them for food. [30]And to every beast of the earth, and to every bird of the air, and to everything that creeps on the earth, everything that has the breath of life, I have given every green plant for food." And it was so. [31]God saw everything that he had made, and indeed, it was very good. And there was evening and there was morning, the sixth day.

[2:1]Thus the heavens and the earth were finished, and all their multitude. [2]And on the seventh day God finished the work that he had done, and he rested on the seventh day from all the work that he had done. [3]So God blessed the seventh day and hallowed it, because on it God rested from all the work that he had done in creation.

[4a]These are the generations of the heavens and the earth when they were created. (Genesis 1:1–2:4a)

The second version of Creation, found in chapter 2, responds to the same primal question, but describes it in a less linear fashion, and the first man and woman take center stage:

[4b]In the day that the Lord God made the earth and the heavens, [5]when no plant of the field was yet in the earth and no herb of the field had yet sprung up—for the Lord God had not caused it to rain upon the earth, and there was no one to till the ground; [6]but a stream would rise from the earth, and water the whole face of the ground— [7]then the Lord God formed man from the dust of the ground, and breathed into his nostrils the breath of life; and the man became a living being. [8]And the Lord God planted a garden in Eden, in the east; and there he put the man whom he had formed. [9]Out of the ground the Lord God made to grow every tree that is

pleasant to the sight and good for food, the tree of life also in the midst of the garden, and the tree of the knowledge of good and evil....

¹⁵The Lord God took the man and put him in the garden of Eden to till it and keep it. ¹⁶And the Lord God commanded the man, "You may freely eat of every tree of the garden; ¹⁷but of the tree of the knowledge of good and evil you shall not eat, for in the day that you eat of it you shall die."

¹⁸Then the Lord God said, "It is not good that the man should be alone; I will make him a helper as his partner." ¹⁹So out of the ground the Lord God formed every animal of the field and every bird of the air, and brought them to the man to see what he would call them; and whatever the man called each living creature, that was its name. ²⁰The man gave names to all cattle, and to the birds of the air, and to every animal of the field; but for the man there was not found a helper as his partner. ²¹So the Lord God caused a deep sleep to fall upon the man, and he slept; then he took one of his ribs and closed up its place with flesh. ²²And the rib that the Lord God had taken from the man he made into a woman and brought her to the man. ²³Then the man said, "This at last is bone of my bones and flesh of my flesh; this one shall be called Woman for out of Man this one was taken."

²⁴Therefore a man leaves his father and his mother and clings to his wife, and they become one flesh. ²⁵And the man and his wife were both naked, and were not ashamed. (Genesis 2:4b–9, 15–25)

It would be worthwhile to compare both stories of Creation. The contradictions, especially the order of Creation, are quite apparent. Yet both stories reflect the strivings of ancient people to bring clarity to the question, "How did we get here?" that clearly obsessed them.

There are many people who believe in the literal accuracy of the Creation stories in Genesis and continue to hold on to these views long after science has suggested otherwise. However, the speculations about the origins of the world that appear in the Hebrew Bible and other ancient literature have no scientific authority. We can applaud the ingenuity of our ancestors' myth making, we can admire the moral and psychological insights of their stories, but it is difficult to hold on to them as literal truth. There is much to be learned from these early tales as allegory, almost nothing in the way of scientific facts.

THE ORIGIN OF RELIGION

Even though many, or even most, adherents of particular religions claim divine origins for their faiths, many manifestations of religion can be traced to more mundane sources.

Religions include a high degree of folk tradition. These traditions predate the establishment of the religions they are associated with today.

For example, the many different ways that Muslim women in the Arab world and in Southeast Asia cover their faces and bodies—some wear burqas, some wear veils, some hijabs, some chadors, each exposing and covering different areas of skin—have more to do with the regional variations in pre-Islamic folk customs than Qur'anic law.

Similar patterns can be found among the various Christian denominations whose origins can each be traced to a particular part of Europe. For example, the Episcopal Church in the United States is derived from the Anglican Communion and the Church of England. Many of the religious regulations of Anglicanism are derived from the folk traditions of the British people.

These folk traditions have been "Christianized," that is to say that a Christian religious meaning has been superimposed on them. For example, hanging candles (and later electric lights) on a pine tree at Christmastime—the Christmas tree—derives from an ancient folk custom, reinvented and reinterpreted as a Christian symbol. At the darkest time of the year, when most of nature seemed to have died, the still-vital evergreen tree was held in special reverence. Subsequently the tree also became a remembrance of the wooden cross upon which Jesus was crucified.

Many of these folk traditions grew up in an age of widespread illiteracy and scientific ignorance. Since people were already practicing these traditions, the early Church kept them and added new Christian meanings. For example, there is clear historical evidence in the New Testament that Jesus was born in ancient Israel in the springtime, not in December, such as the prominent mention of flocks grazing in the fields, which is a phenomenon that occurs in the springtime, not in the winter when sheep were kept indoors. So why is his birthday celebrated in winter? One theory suggests that early Christians continued to celebrate the holiday Sol Invictus, signifying the rebirth of the sun on the shortest day of the year, then considered to be December 25. This pagan practice either had to be eliminated or invested with new meaning. To eliminate the observance of an ancient folk festival was almost impossible. So, according to this theory, the early church decided to co-opt it, adopting it as a celebration of Jesus's birthday.

Nowadays, one can no longer tell that Jesus's birthday was really in the spring. Snow is ever present in yuletide celebrations, which abound in Nativity scenes, sleighs, Santa Claus, and reindeer. The mythology that has developed over the centuries makes Jesus's birthday the winter festival par excellence.

Adjusting the date of an event to better fit the calender is not as unusual as it might sound. Queen Elizabeth II's actual birthday is April 21, but London's weather is particularly variable at the end of April. So the queen's birthday is celebrated with a huge parade in London in June, on a day that good weather can be predicted with much more certainty. George Washington was born on February 22 and Abraham Lincoln on February 12. Now Presidents' Day is observed at a convenient day between the two, always on a Monday or Friday to allow for a three-day weekend.

The relationship between Christmas and Chanukah, both celebrated close to the darkest day of the year, are closer than the rabbis and the church fathers were willing to admit. Both Chanukah and Christmas have been dubbed a "festival of lights," and not without reason. Ancient peoples believed that the sun was dying at the darkest time of the year and that it needed to be restored. Candles, bonfires, yule logs, and the like were used to revivify the sun. And it worked! The days began to get longer.

The Lutheran Church, Episcopal Church, and Presbyterian Church, with origins in Germany, England, and Scotland, respectively, have all carried their folk customs with them as they spread throughout the world, customs that became codified in each church's respective theologies. For example, every Anglican knows that when the Gospel is read, two candle bearers need to accompany the reader. Of course, this custom had more to do with the need to provide light in a dim church than any specifically religious reason. The Roman Catholic Church, with its strong base in Italy, incorporated many religious traditions that are in fact Italian in origin and have little, if anything, to do with theology. We shall deal with how customs have become parts of religious practices in greater detail when we consider the origins of the major Protestant denominations.

Certain Jewish customs are folk ceremonies made Jewish. For example, Jews believe that there is something intrinsically Jewish in the custom of covering mirrors in a house of mourning. However, Scots do the same thing, as do Cajuns in Louisiana.

Rigorous theology and Jewish law frequently stand aside to make room for local customs. There is a classic Jewish story about a traveling salesman whose territory included the tiniest towns in the Jewish Pale of Settlement in Russia, the western area in which most Jews were required to live, at the end of the nineteenth century. He became something of an expert in Jewish worship because his custom was to attend Sabbath morning services in every town that he visited.

One Sabbath morning, he followed his usual custom and went to the local shul for services. At the time of the Torah reading, he noticed a custom that he had not seen before. When approaching the Ark of the Torah, the rabbi bent low and took three steps forward, then he took the Scroll from the Ark. With the Scroll in his arms, the rabbi bent low again, and took three steps backward.

The traveling salesman was surprised. Never had he seen such strange choreography. He turned to the neighbor on his right and asked where the custom arose. That man did not know. So he then turned to his left and asked that man the same question. He, too, did not know the answer.

Both men knew that the rabbi's steps were an important part of the ritual of reading the Torah, but neither knew the origin of this particular custom.

So our commercial traveler turned to a quite elderly gentleman who had been sitting in a place of honor close to the front of the shul. "Oh," said the old man, "that's easy. A chandelier used to hang there!"

WORDS THE SAME, MEANING DIFFERENT

Americans and British speak the same English language, but we frequently call things by different names. We share the same literary heritage. We watch many of the same television shows. We have internalized the different meanings we gave to the same words. Even so, translating from British to American English is something that we do so frequently that it has become automatic. "Lift" becomes "elevator" and when we are talking about an automobile, "boot" becomes "trunk" in American English. In theology, many words sound the same, and even have related meanings. Nevertheless, the ideas they express are often quite different. Religious words can carry with them universes of meaning, based on life experience and folk tradition, as well as theology.

The word "sin" in Hebrew is *chet*, an archery term meaning "to miss the mark." It relates to what we do in our lives. When we miss the mark, we go back and try again. We Jews have internalized this meaning from our High Holy Day liturgy, which encourages us to repent by recognizing that we missed the mark, and urges us to try again.

For most of Christianity, sin is rather an ineluctable part of the human condition, written in the DNA, as it were. This conviction comes from the notion that Adam and Eve sinned in the Garden of Eden, and that everyone since—all of Adam and Eve's descendants—have inherited their original sin. It is only through Jesus, the Savior, that humanity can be redeemed from its sinful state.

COMMON ORIGINS OF IDEAS

Christianity is a product of Jewish Palestine, circa the first century. That time and place were teeming with ideas, articulated by many thinkers and popularizers.

It is not surprising that there are commonalities between Judaism and Christianity. For example, the idea of resurrection was a popular doctrine among the pious rabbinic Pharisees. The aristocratic hereditary priests, called Sadducees, did not believe in bodily resurrection. Both Jews and early Christians were exposed to this notion. Resurrection would become a major idea in the emerging Christianity, even as it receded into the background in Judaism.

Jews and Christians alike were the beneficiaries of earlier religious traditions. Twentieth-century American scholar of mythology and comparative religion Joseph Campbell, in his book *Occidental Mythology*, reminds us that almost all ancient religions shared the idea of the resurrection of a god-king. Dumuzi, Adonis, Attis, and Dionysis all endured a period of torment in the underworld before they rose again. Campbell goes on to point out that in Judaism, however, it is the people who suffer (the enslavement in Egypt), are purified (their passage through the waters of the Red Sea, their forty years in the desert), and are then reborn in the Land of Israel.

Some scholars try to isolate all the instances in which Judaism or Christianity copied one another. In this case, neither religion copied from the other; the resurrection of Jesus reflected existing belief patterns that were pervasive throughout the ancient Near East.

ELIMINATING PAGANISM?

Judaism and Christianity both draw on a font of common experiences. The early church fathers acted consciously and deliberately in trying to eliminate remnant pagan beliefs.

There are pagan traces in Judaism as well. The Hebrew Bible is replete with traces of Babylonian and Canaanite gods, earlier incarnations of the deity, and gods competitive with Yahweh. Its redactor, or editor, frequently obscured references to these pagan gods, but scholars today have been able to discover the original meanings of their names. It is almost as if, in the oral tradition of storytelling, the references were left in to satisfy peoples' needs, while the explicitly pagan elements were "cleansed."

POETIC IMAGES

Every religion, certainly both Judaism and Christianity, faces the problem of literary or poetic figures that have become literalized. Greeting card manufacturers repeatedly use the image of an open ledger as a symbol for Rosh Hashanah. But this is a poetic metaphor, which appears in the High Holy Day liturgy. Do Jews really believe that God has an accounts book in which are written the deeds of all human beings?

In Christianity, Jesus is sometimes completely conflated with God. Does incarnation literally mean that God is Jesus? Or that Jesus is God? Is this poetry or doctrine, imagery or philosophical idea? It's sometimes hard to tell the difference. And what does "Father, Son, and Holy Spirit" really mean? Interpretations abound. The poetry often takes over from theology, and becomes the theology.

CROSS-CULTURAL BORROWING

There are rampant examples of cross-cultural borrowing throughout Judaism and Christianity. Candles have been used in the Roman Catholic Church for centuries as a way of remembering the dead. In the Middle Ages, Jews began to copy this custom, lighting Yahrzeit candles on the anniversary of the death of a parent or spouse and on Yom Kippur eve.

Jews and Christians lived side by side in the ancient Near East, in Europe, and in the rest of the world and drew on the same cultural traditions. Theologians and clergy do not decide which folk traditions people include in their religious life. But once they are present, the theologians and clergy interpret them according to their religious perspective. As noted above, they frequently take on a life of their own.

IDEAS DIE SLOWLY

Since Vatican II in the 1960s, both the Roman Catholic Church and many Protestant churches have sought to depict Jews and Judaism in a new light. Stunned by the horrors of the Holocaust, many Christians have reexamined their attitudes toward Jews. Doctrines such as Jewish deicide (the charge that Jews were responsible for Jesus's crucifixion, and hence killing God) and replacement theology (the doctrine that the Christian faith superseded God's covenant with the Jews) have been eliminated by many Christian denominations. But an edict from the Vatican or a resolution by delegates at a convention cannot, in one moment, change attitudes and ideas that were developed over centuries.

We are beginning a new era of Christian-Jewish relationships. Jesus's Jewishness has been newly recognized and

21

appreciated by most Christian denominations. There have been important, positive steps forward, but the beliefs and prejudices that have been inculcated since childhood, generation after generation, are stubbornly persistent; they cannot be eliminated with the stroke of a pen. Only time and education can take care of that.

Our goal in this book is to give Jews an understanding of the wide spectrum of the changes in Christianity, and to equip them with the tools they need to appreciate the varieties of Christian thought and practice.

We will also try to neutralize the worst deterrents to better Jewish–Christian understanding by clarifying and disentangling the threads of Christian and Jewish ideas that have become knotted together. While we will make every effort to acknowledge the common origins of Judaism and Christianity, we will also show how each religion took distinctly different paths. We will also look at the folk customs that underlie the practice of both Judaism and Christianity and show how they are related to each other. Certain patterns have always existed in Christian thought. With the exception of rare events like the Second Vatican Council, which few people could have predicted, these patterns are likely to continue into the future. So I shall also gaze into my crystal ball and offer a few hesitant predictions.

2

SIN

MANY JEWS AND CHRISTIANS HAVE WRITTEN about the differences between Judaism and Christianity. Some have suggested that it's all about Jesus and the fact that Jews have not accepted Jesus as the Messiah. While this difference is important, it does not tell the whole story.

On a country road where I frequently drive, there is a sign that reads "Christ Died for Our Sins—1 Corinthians 15:3." The entire verse from this New Testament letter of Paul says: "For I handed on to you as of first importance what I in turn had received: that Christ died for our sins in accordance with the scriptures." For many Christians, this verse summarizes their belief in the divinity of Jesus and affirms their belief in vicarious atonement, that Jesus died to atone for our sins.

> The word "sin" is for Judaism a word of judgment about human action rather than a description of fate. Man, who can choose for or against God, creates sin and thereby assumes responsibility for it. He is the victim of his own deeds.
>
> Leo Baeck,
> *The Essence of Judaism*, p. 162

Judaism and Christianity view the human condition in totally different ways. Classical Christian theology maintains that all human beings are inherently sinful because of Adam's defiance of God in the Garden of Eden, when he ate the fruit from the tree of the knowledge of good and evil.

> [8]They heard the sound of the Lord God walking in the garden at the time of the evening breeze, and the man and his wife hid themselves from the presence of the Lord God among the trees of the garden. [9]But the Lord God called to the man, and said to him, "Where are you?" [10]He said, "I heard the sound of you in the garden, and I was afraid, because I was naked; and I hid myself." [11]He said, "Who told you that you were naked? Have you eaten from the tree of which I commanded you not to eat?" [12]The man said, "The woman whom you gave to be with me, she gave me fruit from the tree, and I ate." [13]Then the Lord God said to the woman, "What is this that you have done?" The woman said, "The serpent tricked me, and I ate." [14]The Lord God said to the serpent, "Because you have done this, cursed are you among all animals and among all wild creatures; upon your belly you shall go, and dust you shall eat all the days of your life. [15]I will put enmity between you and the woman, and between your offspring and hers; he will strike your head, and you will strike his heel." [16]To the woman he said, "I will greatly increase your pangs in childbearing; in pain you shall bring forth children, yet your desire shall be for your husband, and he shall rule over you." [17]And to the man he said, "Because you have listened to the voice of your wife, and have eaten of the tree about which I commanded you, 'You shall not eat of it,' cursed is the ground because of you; in toil you shall eat of it all the days of your life; [18]thorns and thistles it shall bring forth for you; and you shall eat the plants of the field. [19]By the sweat of your face

you shall eat bread until you return to the ground, for out of it you were taken; you are dust, and to dust you shall return." (Genesis 3:8–19)

The Garden of Eden myth that ancient peoples created attempts to further explain how the world was created and how men and women came to be, the presence of evil in the world, why women suffer pain in childbirth, why snakes don't have legs, and why life is so tough for most people.

Many Christians and some Jews accept the ingenious stories that are recounted in the early chapters of Genesis as historically accurate statements that describe exactly how things occurred. We will deal in depth with literalist interpretations of the Bible in a later chapter.

Oʀɪɢɪɴᴀʟ Sɪɴ

Human sinfulness stands at the heart of the Christian view of the world. This concept is called original sin.

At its simplest, original sin expresses a worldview that people are inherently sinful and need to be redeemed. *Original sin* is not found as such in the New Testament,

> If Christ alone is He in whom all men are justified, on the ground that it is not simply the imitation of His example which makes men just, but His grace which regenerates men by the Spirit, then also Adam is the only one in whom all have sinned, on the ground that it is not the mere following of his evil example that makes men sinners, but the penalty which generates through the flesh.
>
> St. Augustine "On Merit and the Forgiveness of Sins, and the Baptism of Infants" (Book I), Chapter 19

though it does include key passages (such as Romans 5:12, 19) on which St. Augustine of Hippo, a church father who lived in North Africa from 354 to 430, based the doctrine. Augustine asserted that as a result of Adam's defiance of God, all human beings are born into a state of sin.

According to Christian professor of theology Alistair McFadyen in his book *Bound to Sin*, "sin enters the world through a particular human being's [Adam's] free decision to turn away from God. This is *the* original sin. Second, all subsequent generations of human beings inherit the consequences of this first sin."[1]

> Christ is the suffering servant of God, and so was Job. In the case of Christ the sins of the world are the cause of suffering, and the suffering of the Christian is the general answer. This leads inescapably to the question: Who is responsible for these sins? In the final analysis it is God who created the world and its sins, and who therefore became Christ in order to suffer the fate of humanity.
>
> Carl Gustav Jung,
> *Memories, Dreams, Reflections*, p. 216

Augustine asserted that the cleansing rite of baptism had the power to remove this sinfulness, to wash it away. As a result, for some Christian traditions, the ritual of baptism, whether for infants or adults, is much more than a symbolic Christian rite. It is a crucial, salvific experience. Other Christian traditions view baptism differently. For them, baptism is "a sign and a seal" of the saving work that God has *already* done in the life of the believer and marks the beginning of participation in Christian community.

Baptism is the Christianization of an ancient traditional Jewish ritual. Water cleansing is described in the Hebrew Bible in the story of Elisha and Naaman, in which Naaman is cured of leprosy by immersing himself in the Jordan River (2 Kings 5). Certainly in the period of the Second Temple (500 BCE to 70 CE), increasing importance was accorded to ritual cleansing. The Essenes, a Jewish sect that lived near the Dead Sea and who are the source of the famous Dead Sea Scrolls, were frequent practitioners of ritual immersion for purity's sake. Some of them even began each day with a ritual bath.

New religions frequently adopt customs from earlier religious traditions to authenticate their beliefs, and the early Christians, many Jewish in their origins, were no exception. Emulating the Jewish practice of ritual immersion as a sign of conversion and of repentance from sin, Christians made baptism the principle initiation rite of their new religion.

Despite its Jewish origin, baptism evokes extremely negative collective memories for many Jews. While forced baptism is no longer practiced or condoned by the Catholic Church, there have been numerous incidents throughout history where Jewish children, in particular, were literally stolen from their parents and were baptized and raised as Christians. One of the most famous cases is that of Edgar Mortara, who was secretly baptized by a Christian servant in Bologna, Italy, in 1858. By Vatican law he was seized, taken to a monastery, and raised as a Christian. In spite of every effort by his parents, and an international outcry, he was never returned to his family. Taken under the personal protection of the pope, Mortara ultimately became a Catholic priest.

The history of the Inquisition in Spain and Portugal in the fourteenth and fifteenth centuries is filled with examples of Jews, who, threatened with expulsion, starvation, or violence, submitted to baptism.

Despite the tainted history of the practice, the Jewish version of water cleansing for religious purposes is still in existence. Many converts to Judaism are immersed in a *mikvah*, a special ritual bath, to seal their membership in the Jewish religious community. Many Orthodox Jews, especially women after the completion of their menstrual periods and after childbirth, visit the *mikvah* for cleansing before resuming sexual relations with their husbands. Some pious Hasidic Jewish men also visit the ritual bath before the onset of the Sabbath and on other occasions.

For John, who baptized Jesus, and for many of Jesus's early followers, ritual cleansing became a token of admission into their faith.

Many Christians today believe that infants should be baptized, but many others, most notably Baptists, believe that this rite is not appropriate for infants, but only for those mature enough to know and understand the essential tenets of their religion.

Not all Christians agreed with Augustine's view of human sinfulness. One of the most interesting chapters in the history of early Christianity concerns Pelagius, who was born in Britain circa 354 and later moved to Rome. In very Jewish terms, Pelagius asserted that people are born with no bias for good or evil, and that the actions of Adam in the Garden of Eden have no influence on the subsequent human condition. He went on to say that ultimately, not only do people have free will, whether they are Christian or heathen, but also that they are capable of choosing God without any extraordinary help. In short, humans basically make their own salvific choices. The church fathers thought, to the contrary, that even the desire to please God was itself a divine gift, so that every human choice relied upon God for its freedom and integrity. As a result, the church fathers worked long and hard to stamp out what came to be called the Pelagian heresy.

Later, in the twelfth century in France, scholastic philosopher Peter Abelard questioned the proposition that people inherited an essential sin, which they played no role in committing. Abelard also denied that Jesus died for the vicarious atonement of this original sin. (See the chapter following on Jesus for further discussion of this issue.)

Although the doctrine of original sin has been questioned throughout the ages, baptism remains an indispensable precondition for salvation for many Christians today, as it makes concrete one's acceptance of Jesus as the Messiah, Redeemer, and Savior.

Very frequently, religious attitudes are enshrined in literature and in the general attitudes of people, without the benefit of theologians to certify and refine their views. Dante Alighieri, who lived in the late thirteenth and early fourteenth century, in Florence, Italy, was the author of "The Divine Comedy," considered to be one of the great masterpieces of Western literature. While it is not a theological document, this poem captures the popular views of his Christian contemporaries.

"The Divine Comedy" poem depicts the various stages of hell, purgatory, and paradise. Like much of world literature, this work has entered the collective consciousness, either through actual study or by cultural osmosis. The presence and nature of hell in the religious thinking of many people comes from Dante's work, whether he enshrined folktales from the past or invented new ones of his own.

For many Christians today, original sin is an inescapable fact of life and hell is a reality where those sinners who do not accept Jesus as their Savior may end up. Many other Christians, however, do not believe in a literal hell, and affirm that becoming a Christian is not about avoiding hell, but rather about actively choosing a particular path for following God.

SATAN

From the beginning of time, people have wondered about the origins of evil in the world. Though storytellers, philosophers, and believers have all ventured their own explanations, our curiosity has never been satisfied.

For some, evil has its origin in Satan. Mythology identifies the snake in the Garden of Eden story as Satan. In various religions that coexisted with ancient Judaism in the Middle East, the snake took on an ominous role as an opposition force to the will of the gods.

In the Hebrew Bible and in later religious literature, especially in the Midrash and Talmud, as well as in the Kabbalah, Satan becomes the accuser, like a prosecutor in court. This is the role that Satan plays in the biblical book of Job. He is the doubter who challenges God in order to prove that Job will remain faithful even if he is afflicted with the loss of his family, property, and health. In many folktales, Satan plays the role of trickster.

In other religious traditions, and in some conservative strands of Christianity, Satan takes on a much larger role. He is the personification of evil, just as God is the personification of good. Another manifestation of Satan is Lucifer, a sort of anti-angel. While most religious traditions are careful to keep Satan on a different level than God, who is at the pinnacle, Satan still plays an important role in their world.

SIN IN THE WORLD

Jews do not ascribe evil or sin to Satan. For Jews, evil comes from the behavior of human beings themselves. They have the capacity to do good as well.

See, I have set before you today life and prosperity,
death and adversity. If you obey the commandments of
the Lord your God that I am commanding you today, by
loving the Lord your God, walking in his ways, and
observing his commandments, decrees, and ordinances,
then you shall live and become numerous, and the Lord
your God will bless you in the land that you are entering
to possess. But if your heart turns away and you do not
hear, but are led astray to bow down to other gods and
serve them, I declare to you today that you shall perish; you
shall not live long in the land that you are crossing the
Jordan to enter and possess. I call heaven and earth to witness against you today that I have set before you life and
death, blessings and curses. Choose life so that you and
your descendants may live, loving the Lord your God,
obeying him, and holding fast to him; for that means life
to you and length of days, so that you may live in the land
that the Lord swore to give your ancestors, to Abraham, to
Isaac, and to Jacob.

Deuteronomy 30:15–20

As we have already seen, the Hebrew word that is translated as "sin" is *chet*, a term from archery meaning "to miss the
mark." Another Hebrew word for sin is *avera*. *Avera* can also
be translated as "transgression." This nonbiblical term has as
its root the word *avar*, which means "to pass through, or pass
over, into a different state."

The liturgy for Yom Kippur, the Jewish Day of
Atonement, reminds us of the Jewish notion of sin and repen-
tance. In the alternate Torah reading for the morning of the
Day of Atonement, the book of Deuteronomy, chapter 30,

articulates the message that people have the choice to do good. (This, by the way, is not the traditional Bible reading, but rather one substituted by the authors of many theologically liberal Jewish prayer books.) The newly chosen passage reads: "I call heaven and earth to witness against you this day that I have set before you life or death, blessing or curse; choose life, therefore, that you and your descendants may live—by loving the Lord your God, listening to God's voice, and holding fast to the One who is your life and the length of your days."[2]

And from the Reform movement's prayer book itself:

You are a God of forgiveness: gracious and merciful, endlessly patient, loving and true. You ask evil doers to return to You, and do not seek their death; for it has been said: "Declare to them: As I live, says the Lord God, it is not the death of the wicked I seek, but that they turn from their ways and live. Turn back, turn back from your evil ways; for why should you choose to die, O House of Israel?"[3]

The Jewish notions of sin and good and evil are based on the rabbinic notion that everyone has inherent in them the potential to do good and the potential to do evil. The choice is theirs. Stated another way, no one is strictly evil or strictly good. We have absolute free will to be either.

One important modern idea is that of human perfectibility. This optimistic view of humanity is deeply ingrained in liberal Judaism. In his book *Renewing the Covenant*, theologian and rabbi Eugene Borowitz, the dean of liberal Jewish theologians, speaks of the contemporary phenomenon of self-help books and the popularity of psychotherapy. He also implies that the apparent Jewish preoccupation with psychotherapy is not far removed from their optimistic understanding of the human condition. Borowitz writes,

> [*Chata*—sin] stems from the improper use of our abilities, most probably brought on by faulty social, emotional, or intellectual training. Rather than speak of sin and encumber people with disabling guilt, we should understand misbehavior by its complex causation rather than reduce it to a matter of faulty will. We can remedy it by attention to its origins, by personal therapy that will transform its emotional roots.[4]

Borowitz also points out that in eminent Jewish theologian Martin Buber's well-known formulation of I-Thou relationships, Buber ascribes "our evil doing to our refusal to engage in encounter."[5]

SALVATION

While the Jewish understanding of sin and evil in the world is quite clear, and unrelated to the Christian concepts of salvation and original sin, there are Christians who believe that they are doing a great favor to Jews by introducing them to Jesus and his salvific powers.

B ecause of different understandings of shared stories, Jews and Christians also misunderstand why they come to different understandings of Jesus and messianic ideas.

For example, Judaism does not have a teaching of "original sin" per se; it does not presuppose a negative anthropology in which humanity exists in a state of alienation from

> God. Thus it does not require the sacrifice of the Christ to rectify the original breach.
>
> Amy-Jill Levine, *The Misunderstood Jew*, p. 200

Augustinian theology did not end with Augustine. The original sin proposition was further developed in Christian thought by sixteenth-century theologians Martin Luther, who founded Protestantism, and John Calvin, who further developed the movement. In America, the inheritors of Calvinism included the Puritans and the Dutch settlers of New Amsterdam.

Calvin said that the sin of Adam changed the goodness of Creation, and that people are incapable of changing their basic sinful nature. We are predestined, the Calvinists state, so we must rely on the grace of God to be redeemed from sin, and thus saved.

> Therefore original sin is seen to be an hereditary depravity and corruption of our nature diffused into all parts of the soul.
>
> John Calvin, *Christianae Religionis Institutio (Institutes of the Christian Religion)*, Book II, chapter 1.

What people do in their lives (works), Calvin believed, cannot cause or contribute to their salvation. Faith alone is the central ingredient in salvation. This view is widely accepted in many Protestant denominations, such as Methodists and Baptists. A nuanced theological complication occurs, however, when faith itself becomes the very "work" that people must accomplish in order to be saved. Some Christians are beginning to question the classical understanding based on this complication in how the tradition is lived out.

To a very large extent, being saved or salvation is the essential message of Christianity. This is the heart of where Christianity differs from Judaism. If people are inherently sinful, then Jesus's role as Savior becomes crucial. If instead, as Judaism teaches, people are not inherently sinful but are essentially a combination of good and bad (and the role of religion is to help them affirm the good), then Jesus's salvific powers become unnecessary.

3

JESUS

WHO WAS JESUS? In the almost two thousand years since Jesus walked this earth, his life has been the subject of endless speculation. The search for the historical Jesus has been the focus of much Christian scholarship for the last fifty years. Scholars have examined what life was like in ancient Israel, when the Second Temple existed. They have sought to understand the political forces that operated during the oppressive Roman rule. They have examined the relationships between the aristocratic Sadducees and the Roman ruler, and the role that the rabbinic Pharisees played as the party of the people. One group of scholars, the Jesus Seminar, has sought to determine exactly which words in the Gospels were spoken by Jesus himself, and which words were added by others at later times.

It is important to draw a distinction between Jewish and Christian scholars of the Second Temple period and theologians. Today, most of these scholars pride themselves on their objectivity; they have no prior agenda, no faith-based desire to "prove" anything. Theologians who have delved into this period frequently have quite different motivations.

For many centuries, anti-Semitic Christian scholars sought to present Jesus not as a Jew, but in a totally different light, separated from the tradition in which he was raised in ancient Israel. In the changing Christian world in which we live, most Christian scholars are eager to learn more about

Jesus's Jewish heritage and the practices of Judaism in the first century.

One of the most important sources of information about Judaism in this era is the Mishnah, a law code compiled circa 200 CE by Rabbi Judah HaNasi. One of the great scholars of the Mishnah is Jacob Neusner, who has written dozens of books, often in collaboration with Christian colleagues, trying to probe the mysteries of this period.

In addition to the Mishnah, the discovery of the Dead Sea Scrolls has added much to our understanding of the period of the Second Temple. These scrolls were discovered between 1947 and 1956 along the west bank of the Dead Sea, in Qumran, about fifteen miles east of Jerusalem. More than eight hundred scrolls and fragments of scrolls were discovered in eleven caves. Many scholars believe that these documents are representative of the beliefs of the Essenes, an early Jewish monastic sect. Even after almost sixty years of study, scholars have not come close to exhausting the riches found in these texts, and there is still much to learn.

JESUS THE JEW

Some scholars have drawn on Jewish sources to demonstrate that Jesus taught Judaism, and only Judaism, and that it was Paul who really created the new religion of Christianity. Most of the stories about Jesus's life are found in the four Gospels: Matthew, Mark, Luke, and John. None of these four books was written while Jesus was alive. The earliest is the Gospel of Mark, which was written about the year 70, forty years after Jesus died. The contents of these books were compiled by oral tradition. That is, people told and retold the stories of Jesus's life, and they were only written down at a much later date. Most ancient sacred texts were written in this way.

Some Christian scholars have emphasized Christianity's early separation from Judaism, quoting from the New Testament to show that Paul's true intentions were to build on the ruins of Judaism. But the final break between Judaism and Christianity did not take place until long after the time of Paul. Professor Daniel Boyarin of the University of California at Berkeley speaks of the porosity that existed among the Jews and Christians in this period. Professor Wayne A. Meeks of Yale University puts it this way:

> So, obviously they [the Christians] are recognized as a distinctive group. How did this happen? What is involved in their separation? The one thing I think we have to recognize is that it doesn't happen all at once. It does not happen in the same way in different places, nor does it happen at the same time. For example, as late as the 4th and 5th century, we have evidence of Christians still existing within Jewish communities, and we have evidence of members of Christian communities participating in Jewish festivals. The preacher of Antioch and later of Constantinople, John Chrysostom, complains in a series of eight sermons to his congregation, that "you must stop going to the Synagogue, you must not think that the Synagogue is a holier place than our churches are" (Homily XLVII). This clearly indicates that the break between Judaism and Christianity, even as late as the 4th century ... still is not absolute, is not permanent.[1]

Though some Christian scholars disagree, it is clear that Judaism and Christianity did not go their separate ways until the fourth century, when Emperor Constantine signed the Edict of Milan, which established official tolerance of Christianity throughout the Roman Empire.

When Jesus is located within the world of Judaism, the ethical implications of his teachings take on a renewed and heightened meaning; their power is restored and their challenge sharpened. Jews as well as Christians should be able to agree on a number of these teachings today, just as in the first century Jesus's followers and even those Jews who chose not to follow him would have agreed with such basic assertions as that God is our father, that his name should be hallowed, and that the divine kingdom is something ardently to be desired. Conversely, the failure to understand the Jewish Jesus within his Jewish context has resulted in the creation and perpetuation of millennia of distrust, and worse, between church and synagogue.

Amy-Jill Levine, *The Misunderstood Jew*, p. 21

Jesus's Death as Redemption

Among the essential Christian theological assertions about Jesus that Jews need to understand is the idea that Jesus's death on the cross was a redemptive sacrifice for the sins of humanity. Here, Jesus becomes the sacrifice, much as sacrifices were used in the Jewish Temple cult to rid people of sin. This notion of vicarious atonement for human sins stands at the heart of the cosmos for classical Christian teaching.

Radically transformed but never uprooted, the sacrifice of the first-born son constitutes a strange and usually overlooked bond between Judaism and Christianity and thus a major unexplored focus for Jewish-Christian dialogue. In the past, this dialogue has too often centered on the Jewishness of Jesus and, in particular, his putative roles of prophet and sage. In point of fact, however, those roles, even if real, have historically been vastly less important in Christian tradition than Jesus's identity as a sacrificial victim, the son handed over to death by his loving father or the lamb who takes away the sins of the world. This identity, ostensibly so alien to Judaism, was itself constructed from Jewish reflection on the beloved sons of the Hebrew Bible, reflection that long survived the rise of Christianity and has persisted into the post-Holocaust era. The bond between Jewry and the Church that the beloved son constitutes is, however, enormously problematic. For the long-standing claim of the Church that it *supersedes* the Jews in large measure continues the old narrative pattern in which a late-born son dislodges his first-born brothers, with varying degrees of success. Nowhere does Christianity betray its indebtedness to Judaism more than in its supersessionism.

Jon D. Levenson, *The Death and Resurrection of the Beloved Son*, p. x

These ideas about Jesus and his powers were solidified theologically by various church councils from the fourth century onward. This is analogous to the oral tradition that shaped the Talmud and later rabbinic texts, while continually adapting Judaism to contemporary needs.

Scholars now assert that two new religions emerged after the destruction of the Second Temple in the year 70 CE: Rabbinic Judaism and Christianity. Both of these religions draw heavily on the biblical texts, but both also essentially separate themselves from the Bible in important ways.

While the rabbis developed their new religion, what we refer to as Rabbinic Judaism, the church fathers proceeded along similar lines in developing the emerging Christianity, synthesizing Jewish, Greek, and Roman traditions as well as other religious traditions of the ancient Near East. The Roman Catholic Church accepts the same developmental premises as the rabbis. Their understandings of the teachings of Jesus emerged from a continuous process of interpretation that did not end with the canonization of the books that now comprise the official New Testament. Their term for this extracanonical knowledge is the Magisterium, which refers to the common teaching authority of the bishops throughout the life of the Church.

After the Reformation, many Protestant denominations, which separated themselves from the authority of the pope, articulated the principle that each person is capable of his or her individual interpretation of scripture, with or without the benefit of the knowledge of what ideas or interpretations went before them. This is how some popular views of Jesus, often seemingly absurd or inappropriate—for instance, when his words are interjected into political campaigns, or used to help advertise get-rich-quick swindles—came to be. Many Christians understand that these interpretations stray very far from the original biblical text.

Yet Christian understandings of who Jesus was do vary, and sometimes widely. Was he a rebel or a quietist? A radical or a conservative? Pro- or anti-business?

For some contemporary scholars, Jesus is studied as a Jew who lived in a Jewish environment in ancient Israel two thousand years ago. There are theologians who forcibly wrench Jesus out of the Jewish world into which he was born, and regard him as beginning a completely new chapter in human history. Others see Jesus as a spinner of tales and parables, a natural teacher, and an inspiring humanist. For others Jesus is the latest avatar of the many resurrected gods in mythology, including Adonis, Osiris, and Dionysus. And for still others, he is the Son of God, begotten not made, of one being with the Father, who will come again in glory to judge the living and the dead.

THE VIRGIN BIRTH

In the ancient world, the birth of a special teacher or leader was a matter of considerable interest. Perhaps in order to give extra authenticity to their words and underline their superiority, frequent claims of active divine involvement in the birth process were made. Achilles was the son of the divine nymph Thetis and the human king Peleus, and Aeneas was the son of the goddess Aphrodite and the mortal Anchises. Even the birth of Moses, described in Exodus, has magical connotations, especially in Moses's being miraculously rescued from execution and drowning to be the future savior of the Jewish people.

> The notion of the virginal conception of Jesus, developed in the infancy narratives of the gospels, signified an understanding of Jesus as God's elect from his mother's womb—that is, his coming was through divine not human agency. Yet Matthew's tracing of Jesus's genealogy from Abraham and David to Joseph was constructed by a writer who assumed Joseph's paternity (1:2–16).
>
> Rosemary Radford Ruether, *Goddesses and the Divine Feminine*, pp. 150–151

Jesus's birth is described in only two of the Gospels: Matthew and Luke.

[18]Now the birth of Jesus the Messiah took place in this way. When his mother Mary had been engaged to Joseph, but before they lived together, she was found to be with child from the Holy Spirit. [19]Her husband Joseph, being a righteous man and unwilling to expose her to public disgrace, planned to dismiss her quietly. [20]But just when he had resolved to do this, an angel of the Lord appeared to him in a dream and said, "Joseph, son of David, do not be afraid to take Mary as your wife, for the child conceived in her is from the Holy Spirit. [21]She will bear a son, and you are to name him Jesus, for he will save his people from their sins." [22]All this took place to fulfil what had been spoken by the Lord through the prophet: [23]"Look, the virgin shall conceive and bear a son, and they shall name him Emmanuel," which means, "God is with us." [24]When Joseph awoke from sleep, he did as the angel of the Lord commanded him; he took her as his wife, [25]but had no marital relations with her until she had borne a son; and he named him Jesus. (Matthew 1:18–25)

[26]In the sixth month the angel Gabriel was sent by God to a town in Galilee called Nazareth, [27]to a virgin engaged to a man whose name was Joseph, of the house of David. The virgin's name was Mary. [28]And he came to her and said, "Greetings, favored one! The Lord is with you." [29]But she was much perplexed by his words and pondered what sort of greeting this might be. [30]The angel said to her, "Do not be afraid, Mary, for you have found favor with God. [31]And now, you will conceive in your womb and bear a son, and you will name him Jesus. [32]He will be great, and will be called the Son of the Most High, and the Lord God will give to him the throne of his ancestor

David. ³³He will reign over the house of Jacob for ever, and of his kingdom there will be no end." ³⁴Mary said to the angel, "How can this be, since I am a virgin?" ³⁵The angel said to her, "The Holy Spirit will come upon you, and the power of the Most High will overshadow you; therefore the child to be born will be holy; he will be called Son of God. ³⁶And now, your relative Elizabeth in her old age has also conceived a son; and this is the sixth month for her who was said to be barren. ³⁷For nothing will be impossible with God." ³⁸Then Mary said, "Here am I, the servant of the Lord; let it be with me according to your word." Then the angel departed from her. (Luke 1:26–38)

Charles H. Talbert, professor of religion at Baylor University in Texas, points out in his book *Reading Acts* that "Luke's material about the birth and early life of Jesus functions within the ancient genre of prophecies of future greatness. Prophecies, portents, and other material foreshadow the future greatness of the child."[2]

Tales about Jesus's miraculous conception and virgin birth are found in the New Testament text, but many scholars argue that this material is a result of the *theological* understanding of the Gospel writers, not a statement of historical fact.

THE TRINITY

The Trinity is among the most difficult Christian concepts for Jews to understand. That is as it should be—it is a mystery and as such, not amenable to rational explanation. Ultimately it is a tenet of faith that affirms the fundamental unity of the Godhead existing in three distinct Persons: the Father, the

Son, and the Holy Spirit. Sometimes the Trinity is roughly compared to the way water can be found in three forms: solid (ice), liquid, and gas (vapor). Not all Christians accept the literal meaning of the Trinity. For some it is allegorical, a way of thinking about how God is manifested on earth.

It was the early church councils that settled the various controversies surrounding the idea of the Trinity. The Council of Nicaea in the fourth century articulated the doctrine most clearly. This is the text, known as the Nicene Creed, which is part of many regular Christian services:

> We believe in one God, the Father, the Almighty, maker of heaven and earth, of all that is, seen and unseen.
>
> We believe in one Lord, Jesus Christ, the only Son of God, eternally begotten of the Father, God from God, Light from Light, true God from true God, begotten, not made, of one Being with the Father. Through him all things were made. For us and for our salvation he came down from heaven: by the power of the Holy Spirit he became incarnate from the Virgin Mary, and was made man. For our sake he was crucified under Pontius Pilate; he suffered death and was buried. On the third day he rose again in accordance with the Scriptures; he ascended into heaven and is seated at the right hand of the Father. He will come again in glory to judge the living and the dead, and his kingdom will have no end.
>
> We believe in the Holy Spirit, the Lord, the giver of life, who proceeds from the Father and the Son. With the Father and the Son he is worshiped and glorified. He has spoken through the Prophets. We believe in one holy catholic and apostolic Church. We acknowledge one baptism for the forgiveness of sins. We look for the resurrection of the dead, and the life of the world to come. Amen.

Many Christian thinkers would maintain that neither the Hebrew Bible nor the New Testament contains any specific reference to the Trinity as a manifestation of God. Some would assert that texts in the New Testament which specifically support the doctrine of the Trinity—such as Jesus' command to baptize in the name of the Father, the Son and the Holy Spirit (Matthew 28:19)—are little better than proof texts. Others would cite the story of the baptism of Jesus in Luke 1 and Matthew 1, where the voice of the Father is heard, the Spirit as a dove is seen, and the person of Jesus is immersed in the water as evidence of this complex doctrine.

Christianity, like Judaism, grew up in a world in which many religious traditions were known to the people. These religious traditions, especially the philosophical mysticism of Greek Neoplatonism, would have a profound influence on Christianity. When the doctrine of the Trinity was adopted by fourth-century Christianity and became part of the Nicene Creed, many objections were voiced, too numerous to mention here. The central importance of this doctrine is revealed in the reason for the split between the Orthodox churches of the East and Western Christianity some five hundred years after the matter had supposedly been settled: the so-called *filioque* (meaning "and the son" in Latin) clause. Where the original Nicene Creed reads "We believe in the Holy Spirit ... who proceeds from the Father," the Roman Catholic Church amended it to say "We believe in the Holy Spirit ... who proceeds from the Father and the Son." The Eastern Church did not accept this addition.

While Christianity is clearly a monotheistic religion, the idea of three distinct Persons in one Godhead has sparked many theological arguments through the centuries. The nature of God, the Father, is fairly clear. The second manifestation, the Son, is more difficult to explain.

GOD BECOMES FLESH (INCARNATION)

For some the figure of Jesus is so mysterious that it can hardly be contemplated. The theology of incarnation is quite complicated and, for many, arcane. The Gospel of John, in the very first chapter, says, "In the beginning was the Word, and the Word was with God, and the Word was God…. And the Word became flesh and lived among us" (John 1:1, 14a). The notion of God (whom John refers to as "the *Logos*," translated from Greek as "the Word") becoming flesh (incarnated) is difficult even for some Christians to understand. Theologians have pondered incarnation through the centuries. Catholic theologians speak of the "hypostatic union of the divine nature and the human nature of Jesus in the divine person of Jesus Christ."[3]

Jews should not assume that any of the doctrines of Christianity that seem to be widely accepted today are easily understood by Christians, nor should Jews assume that the early church was not a place of intense debate about each of these "essential" ideas. Karen Armstrong, in her book *A History of God*, writes about the essence of God and its manifestation in the divinity of Jesus. She makes the point that all religions make the distinction between the esoteric (hidden) and exoteric (plain) truths. The esoteric truths can be found in Judaism and in Islam as well. In Judaism, there were kabbalistic traditions, and in Islam, there were Sufi traditions. Armstrong notes that Basil, one of Christianity's early teachers, called "attention to the fact that not all religious truth was capable of being expressed and defined clearly and logically."[4] The Roman Catholic Church has declared that the idea of the Trinity is a mystery, something "hidden by the veil of faith and enveloped, so to speak, by a kind of darkness."[5]

THE RESURRECTED GOD

So, how is a Jew to understand what our Christian neighbors believe? The answer is not easy. Perhaps it is fair to say that ordinary people, ordinary Jews, and ordinary Christians are less than clear about every aspect of their own religions and theologies.

But we can begin our examination of the nature of Jesus by utilizing an anthropological and psychological approach. Joseph Campbell, the well-known interpreter of human mythology, drew on the work of the Swiss psychiatrist Carl Jung in his classic *Occidental Mythology*. According to this approach, there are basic human myths (essential archetypal stories) that repeat themselves in different guises in every culture. Another of Campbell's books is called *The Hero with a Thousand Faces*, the title of which clearly conveys this theme. Campbell finds parallel instances of the same story over and over again in diverse societies that had no contact with each other. Though overlaid with thin veneers of local characteristics, once one digs past the façade, the same basic story is revealed.

This concept, which Campbell dubbed the monomyth, holds that these myths emerge from common ancient human experiences. It is as if they are not copied from one culture to another, but are a part of the human DNA, which is transmitted from generation to generation.

Campbell points out that many spring festivals celebrate the annual resurrection of divine kings or heroes, such as Dumuzi, Adonis, Attis, and Dionysis. He notes that the resurrection of Jesus came to be celebrated on the same date as the annual festival commemorating the resurrection of Adonis.

As I mentioned earlier, Campbell notes that the spring rebirth festival of Passover commemorates the resurrection of the people of Israel, not the resurrection of an incarnation or manifestation of God.

If Jung's and Campbell's approaches to resurrection are valid, then Jews can appreciate the relationship between the celebration of Easter and the celebration of Passover in a new and sophisticated light.

The facts here are perfectly clear and well-documented: The life of the God-man on earth comes to an end with his resurrection and transition to heaven. This is firm belief since the beginning of Christianity. In mythology it belongs to the hero that conquers death and brings back to life his parents, tribal ancestors, etc. He has a more perfect, richer, and stronger personality than the ordinary mortal. Although he is mortal himself, death does not annihilate his existence: he continues living in a somewhat modified form. On a higher level of civilization he approaches the type of the dying and resurrected god, like Osiris, who becomes a greater personality in every individual (like the Johannine Christ), viz., the complete (or perfect) man, the self.

Carl Gustav Jung, *Psychology and Western Religion*, pp. 248–249

THE LAST SUPPER

The Gospels describe Jesus's Last Supper, which may or may not have been an early version of the Passover seder. Two elements of the seder have been incorporated into Christian worship: the ritual drinking of wine and eating of unleavened bread. The first part of a Catholic Mass, like the Sabbath service in synagogue, is a combination of education and prayer, including scripture readings and the sermon. The Eucharist (which means "thanksgiving" in Greek), or Holy Communion, which corresponds to the Sabbath meal and the Passover seder, is the second part of the service, and it is just for those who are already Christians. In the early church, those who were not yet baptized had to leave the room.

For Catholics, the celebration of Mass changed as a result of Vatican II. Mass was once conducted with the priest's back turned toward the congregation, almost as if they were ignoring those who were to partake of the ceremony. Now, in almost all Roman Catholic churches, the ritual is performed facing the people.

What exactly occurs during the eucharist has long been a source of debate within Christian traditions. In the Roman Catholic Church, while the appearance of the bread and wine do not change, when they are consecrated by the priest they *become* transformed into the body and the blood of Christ, the Messiah. This is called "transubstantiation." Other traditions believe in "consubstantiation," which means the bread and wine are still really bread and wine, but they are simultaneously really the body and blood of Jesus. Still others describe the "Real Presence" of Jesus in the elements in a variety of other ways.

The ultimate question with respect to Jesus is this: Is Jesus the Messiah? While there are passages in the Hebrew Bible, the *Tanakh*, foretelling the coming of the Messiah, most modern Jews interpret this idea as a messianic age of peace and harmony brought about by our own human efforts and not by divine intervention. Since Judaism does not regard the human family as being innately sinful, there is no need for anyone to play a redemptive role in society. This is the essential reason that Jews do not believe they need Jesus in order to be saved.

Jews have moved far away from the sacrificial rituals of the Second Temple. Vestiges of them are more apparent in Roman Catholic and Episcopal churches than in most synagogues, such as the vestments that the clergy wear, as well as Jesus's status as the sacrificial lamb. The synagogue has eschewed vestments for clergy and sacrificial rituals to a very large extent. *Shlugging kaporis* is a folk tradition that is reminiscent of the sacrificial elements of Temple worship. This is when a live chicken is swung about the head and then is cast off, just as sins are to be cast off. Though some ultra-orthodox communities still perform this ritual, it is not part of mainstream Judaism in the twenty-first century.

4

END TIMES

SOME CHRISTIANS IN EVERY DENOMINATION share interest in ideas in which Jews have limited interest, such as one's individual salvation. Much classical Christian theology is built around heaven and hell as places one might end up after death. This is a theme that runs through literature, especially in the Middle Ages. It concerned Dante and Milton, both of whom wrote major works concerned with human sinfulness and the punishments and rewards that await us in the afterlife.

The Jewish concept of salvation cannot be properly understood without considering these significant facts:

(1)   The gates of salvation are open to all men. It is not limited to members of the House of Israel. The righteous among the non-Jews have a place in the world to come. For this reason the seven laws of Noah were given to mankind. While Jews are required to observe 613 commandments, non-Jews can attain salvation merely by observing the seven Noachian commandments, prohibiting idolatry, blasphemy, cursing of judges, murder, incest and adultery, robbery, and the eating of flesh with the blood of life in it....

(2) In keeping with this universalism, certain Jewish thinkers have declared that Christianity and Islam, as Judaism's daughter-religions, have their part to play in the scheme of salvation. They help prepare the soil for the messianic kingdom.…

(3) There is no salvation in Judaism by faith alone or by the mere acceptance of a creed. Nor is there salvation attained by mediation. God freely remits the sin of the penitent. As a result of each man's awareness of the manner of life required by God, the whole world will awaken to the demands of the higher life. Salvation will be complete when "the earth shall be full of the knowledge of the Lord, as the waters cover the sea." (Isaiah 11:9)

Abraham Shusterman in *The Universal Jewish Encyclopedia*, vol. 9, pp. 332–333

Just as there is a concern for the fate of individuals after their deaths, there is a similar concern for what will happen to the world at the end of time. For Jews, the idea is expressed in the phrase *y'mot ha-mashiach* ("the days of the Messiah"), whenever that might be. But the Jewish focus has never been on the end of one's days, or on the end of the world. The emphasis has always been on making our lives and our world a better place. The Messiah is often understood less as a persona and more as a time of peace and harmony.

Other terms in Judaism that refer to the end times are *sheol* and *Gehennom*. *Sheol* is the place where the dead reside, where souls are perhaps cut off from God. No one praises him there, according to Psalm 6:5. *Gehennom* is a more common term. It literally refers to a physical place outside

Jerusalem, the Valley of Henom, meaning the Valley of Nothing. There was considerable conflict in Jewish thinking, especially during the period of the Second Temple, when most of the New Testament was written. The Sadducees, the priestly aristocrats, rejected any notion of heaven or hell. The Pharisees, the group representing ordinary people, regarded *Gehennom* as an eternal prison, where the wicked would remain after death. The Essenes, a mystical sect, believed in the immortality of the soul.

The highly influential writings of Maimonides, who lived in twelfth-century Spain, asserted that *Gehennom* is a figure of speech, not to be taken literally. But one of Maimonides' thirteen tenets of faith states that the dead will be bodily resurrected when the Messiah comes.

Even so, most Jews only pay lip service to the idea of life after death. In contrast, the Jewish concept of *tikkun olam*, "repairing the world," has been around for centuries and most clearly articulates the view that what happens here and now is of paramount importance. *Tikkun olam*, while stated in theological terms, has an immediacy and practicality: Our job on earth, Judaism says, is to perfect God's creation.

This concept is the basis for the Jewish emphasis on social justice, which has found a home in American Reform Judaism in particular. But Reform Jews aren't the only ones embracing this cause. Abraham Joshua Heschel, who was a professor at the Conservative movement's Jewish Theological Seminary and one of the leading Jewish thinkers of our time, marched with Rev. Martin Luther King, Jr., on more than one occasion during the 1950s and '60s, and spoke out courageously on the war in Vietnam as well.

Jews were deeply concerned with civil rights in many ways that were not necessarily religious. The great Oscar Hammerstein and Richard Rodgers, both Jewish, taught the lesson of *tikkun olam* in their 1949 musical *South Pacific*, particularly in the anti-racism song "You've Got to Be Taught," which they were begged to omit because it would not be appreciated in certain quarters of the United States.[1]

Perfecting the world through our actions is so ingrained in the Jewish way of thinking that it is a major preoccupation of even nonreligious Jews. Thus Jews have a hard time understanding the complexities of Christian end-times theology, but let us turn our attention to it now.

THE BOOK OF REVELATION

The New Testament book of Revelation is the key document that Jews need to know about when trying to understand the Christian view of the end times, a field of study known as eschatology. Revelation (not Revelations) is the last book of the New Testament. It was written about the year 96 CE and its authorship is attributed to John the Elder, whose origins are in the city of Ephesus in what is now Turkey.

Before we proceed further, I should provide a caveat and emphasize that by no means do all Christians subscribe to belief in the end times as described below. The popularity of sensational books such as the *Left Behind* series notwithstanding, many Christians view the book of Revelation within the larger tradition of biblical prophecy (which was less concerned with forecasting the future than about calling for social justice in the here and now, as described below), and view predicting the Second Coming of Jesus and other end times events as secondary in importance to living a life marked by social justice and love of neighbor.

Revelation is filled with complicated symbols and imagery, such as monstrous beasts, fiery thrones, and bloody battles among supernatural armies, with which most modern

Americans—much less Jews—are quite unfamiliar. However, it is important to point out that much of that imagery and language is drawn from the Hebrew Bible, especially the books of Daniel, Ezekiel, and Zechariah, although Revelation moves in an entirely different direction from Jewish prophetic literature.

Professor Marc Zvi Brettler of Brandeis University writes in his book *How to Read the Bible*, "The main purpose of classical prophecy was *not* to predict the future. Prophets do spend a lot of time talking about the future, but they do so for two reasons. One reason is to convince people to repent. The second reason is that if Israel suffers, it means that God has judged and punished them for their covenant infractions."[2]

As mentioned above, many Christians view the book of Revelation in light of the larger biblical prophetic tradition, seeing it as a message of hope to early Christians that God would prevail over their persecutors in Rome—not through violence, but by overturning violence. Many other Christians, however—particularly high-profile preachers and writers who receive the lion's share of media attention—emphasize the apocalyptic aspects of Revelation, how the end of the world will come about. An all-out war between the forces of good and evil is described. Jesus will come to reign for a thousand years. Satan, contained for this period of time, will reemerge, but ultimately be conquered by Jesus. There are only twenty-two chapters in Revelation; though it is difficult, it is worthwhile reading this book in its entirety to understand the background for Christian end-time predictions.

Since the turn of the millennium, much Christian attention has been focused on the potential for worldwide calamity. Some eschatologically-minded Christians have asserted that the Iraq war is an example of an armageddon, a great war between the forces of good and evil, as was predicted in Revelation.

Since the imagery in Revelation is so visceral and concrete, yet at the same time highly symbolic, there is much leeway for creative interpretation, particularly for readers who do not use historical-critical methods of interpretation. Such readers often see Revelation's symbolic references as applying to current and future geopolitical events. Some television preachers, as well as their counterparts in church pulpits all over America, take this liberty.

FUNDAMENTALISM

Christian fundamentalism is largely an American phenomenon. It grew up in the early part of the twentieth century as a response to the growth of a highly rationalist approach to Christianity that questioned every aspect of Christian belief, sought freedom from creeds and traditional dogmas, and wanted the freedom to read the Bible and question it as any other historical or literary text.

In response to this modernist approach, in 1910 the newly called fundamentalists began publishing a twelve-volume set of essays that purported to refute modern theology and set forth the *fundamentals* of the Christian faith. Their new movement sought to save Christianity from what it believed to be an erosion in traditional belief and at the same time to set forth a new orthodoxy or right practice for Christians.

The fundamental doctrines asserted were:

1. The verbal literal inerrancy of scripture
2. The divinity of Jesus
3. The virgin birth
4. Vicarious atonement
5. The physical resurrection and bodily return of Jesus

The modernist (rationalist) approach to Christianity—which is still alive and well in America—was quite congenial to the thinking of most educated Jews. Scientific biblical criticism was already widely accepted by Reform and Conservative Jews, and in some ways even by modern Orthodox Jews as well. The Jewish emphasis on learning and knowledge also ran counter to the fundamentalists, who emphasized the dangers of "too much education."

Another important contributor to the fundamentalist backlash against modernism was the rise of a popular but controversial movement called dispensationalism, led by a British evangelist named John Nelson Darby in the latter part of the nineteenth century in England. Dispensationalists believe that human history is divided into seven different time periods (or dispensations), in which God has dealt differently with human beings. These eras are the Garden of Eden, Adam to Noah, Noah to Abraham, Abraham to Moses, Moses to Jesus, Jesus to Judgment Day, and the millennial kingdom.

> You have to take Biblical prophecy literally, just like everything else in the Bible.
>
> Tim LaHaye, interview with www.family christian.com

Dispensationalists believe that Jesus will return to earth before the world actually comes to an end and will reign for a thousand years, hence they are also called millennialists. This return of Jesus is called the Second Coming or Last Coming. Sometimes the Greek term *parousia* (meaning "appearance and subsequent presence with") is used.

Dispensationalists believe that, prior to Jesus's thousand-year reign, the there will be a "rapture," in which all born-again Christians (here understood to be those who have accepted Jesus as their personal Lord and Savior) will be taken up into the sky, followed by the "tribulation," in which the apocalypse will take place. The period of the apocalypse will be marked by terrible devastation from which only born-again Christians will be saved. After the period of destruction has ended, those who were spirited away in the rapture will return to earth.

This particularly dispensationalist understanding of the end times is the fundamental theological framework found in the *Left Behind* series of books. It is worth noting again that dispensational teaching, while popular, is by no means accepted by all Christians, particularly those in mainline denominations.

Left Behind

A phenomenon that baffles people who don't know about millennialism and dispensationalism is the spectacular success of the *Left Behind* series of novels, cowritten by Tim LaHaye and Jerry B. Jenkins. The books, which have sold tens of millions of copies, describe the horrors of the apocalypse. Jesus returns to earth and establishes his thousand-year reign, but all is not well. Lucifer, the anti-Christ, returns to impose the kingdom of darkness. All of these events, needless to say, are inspired by the book of Revelation and other dispensationalist teachings.

The eschatological narrative of the *Left Behind* series (and of dispensationalism in general) includes one element that Jews should find disquieting. Rabbi Michael J. Cook, author of *Modern Jews Engage the New Testament: Enhancing Jewish Well-Being in a Christian Environment* (Jewish Lights) and professor of intertestamental and early Christian literatures at the Hebrew Union College-Jewish Institute of Religion, has commented that "the series' underlying premise is that, had the Jews accepted Jesus in the first century, God would never have created the Church, which has now lasted 2,000 years purely as a stopgap measure until the Jews accept Jesus." Dr. Cook goes on to say that what this really means is that "the onus for the delay in completing Jesus's work is implicitly held to rest upon the Jews."[3]

This theology is now a part of the popular culture for millions of Christians. Many of them believe that the Second Coming of Jesus is dependent on the conversion of the Jews to Christianity. Thus, Christian Zionism, with its emphasis on Jewish conversion, has become an important factor in the interfaith landscape of America. This phenomenon will be discussed further in a later chapter.

EVANGELICALS

The growth of evangelicalism in the 1940s—most visibly in the person of the popular preacher Billy Graham—was a reaction to the intolerance and extremism that had begun to characterize fundamentalism. The evangelicals sought to return conservative Protestantism to the mainstream of American cultural and political life, and in many ways they have succeeded. Most significant is their development of what has become known as the megachurches, in which all kinds of social services are added to the specifically religious program of the church. Their worship services, typically free of traditional ritual, have become high in entertainment value. Rock, country, hip-hop and other popular music genres supplement or supplant organ-accompanied hymns. The sermons emphasize self-help and positive thinking, picking up the themes of preachers like the late Norman Vincent

Peale and others who were star attractions in the mid-twentieth century. Energetic preaching, which seems to have waned in importance in synagogues and mainstream Protestant churches, has found a home in these megachurches. Robert Schuler, Rick Warren, and Joel Osteen, examples of popular preachers from different generations, easily fill large arenas around the United States.

But even though today's evangelicals are less isolated and less separatist than they once were, they continue to look upon secular society with disapproval. Their abhorrence for what they regard as sinful, godless Western secular values is at the heart of many of the political battles being fought in the United States today.

This sense of distrust of modern secular values is a theme that runs through parts of Islam, Judaism, and other Christian traditions as well. Right-wing Islamic clerics have condemned contemporary Western values as represented by the "Great Satan," the United States. Pope Benedict XVI has often stated that Europe must be "re-Christianized." This might be interpreted as a desire to return the Roman Catholic Church to a newly preeminent role or, perhaps, to return to halcyon days when the Church had a great deal more to say about the issues that concern Europeans than it does now. Some Hasidic Jewish sects do not even accept the existence of the state of Israel as it was created without the coming of the Messiah.

"End of days" theology dominates the theology of conservative American Protestantism. Its message, simply stated, is that if you do not accept Jesus as your personal Savior, then you are doomed to burn in hell at the end of days—which might come sooner than you realize.

It is remarkable to note the extraordinary reticence of the Bible and the Mishnah on the subjects of death, resurrection, immortality, the Hereafter, the Judgment Day in the afterlife, Heaven and Hell, and the Messiah—subjects which occupied so large a place in the religions of the Near East, the Greco-Roman world, and Christianity. Resurrection is mentioned once in the Mishnah, when it is announced as a dogma; again, when it is stated that "we make mention of the Power of Rain in the second of Eighteen Benedictions—the Resurrection of the Dead," and once again in the statement of R. Phineas b. Yair that the Holy Spirit leads to the resurrection of the dead and that the latter will come through Elijah. There are no descriptions of the world to come in the Mishnah, and none of the symbolic trivia characteristic of an apocalypse.

Abba Hillel Silver,
Where Judaism Differed, p. 166

5

IS THE BIBLE TRUE?

EVEN A CASUAL VISITOR to a synagogue on a Sabbath morning can immediately see the reverence with which Jews regard the Bible. At the front of every synagogue is the Ark, which holds Torah scrolls, which contain the Five Books of Moses. A portion of the Torah, called the *parasha*, is read on every Sabbath and holy day, followed by an additional reading from another part of the Hebrew Bible. This additional reading, the *haftarah*, carries the same core message as the Torah portion. The custom of the additional reading originated during the reign of Antiochus IV, ruler of the Hellenistic Seleucid Empire, when Jews were forbidden to read from the Torah itself.

Before the reading, the Torah is paraded through the synagogue. People reach out to symbolically kiss the scroll using their prayer books or the fringes of their tallit (prayer shawl). When the reading is concluded, the Scroll is lifted high for all to see.

As much as the Bible is revered in the synagogue, Jews do not read the Bible seeking its literal meaning. Since the fall of the Second Temple in Jerusalem in 70 CE, almost two thousand years of Jewish religious life has been devoted to understanding the message of the Bible in contemporary terms. One of the long-lived traditions is to study the Bible with a multivolume set of commentaries called *Mikraot Gedolot*. Looking much like pages of the Talmud, *Mikraot*

Gedolot contains the Hebrew biblical text surrounded by commentaries drawn from several centuries of Jewish biblical scholars, including Rashi, Abraham ibn Ezra, Gersonides, David Kimhi, Nahmanides, and Sforno. Also included is a translation of the biblical text into Aramaic, known as *Targum*. These books were first published in the sixteenth century.

Jews were encouraged to always read the Bible along with the commentaries so that their understanding of the text could be enhanced by centuries of great scholarship. There was a tacit, but clear, understanding that a person should not depend alone upon one's own individual inter-pretation, which might or might not be valid.

Throughout the centuries, Jewish and Christian schol-ars alike have recognized that there are a number of problems in the biblical text, especially if it was considered to be dic-tated by God to Moses. Among the questions raised were repetitions in the text, such as the account of Creation in Genesis, right at the beginning, which offers two versions of the same story, with a different order of events. Or the fact that Moses reports his own death at the end of the book of Deuteronomy. Also, in one place it might be reported that the Midianites did something, and in another place, the same event is reported as being done by the Moabites.

The rabbis sought to rationalize all of the contradictions in their commentaries. They did this successfully some of the time but not all of the time. Lingering suspicion remained that when there are two versions of the same story, there might have been two documents that were merged together, and not always smoothly.

It was in the nineteenth century, in Germany, that one towering biblical scholar set forth a theory, building on the work of many earlier scholars, that the entire text of the Five Books of Moses was compiled from various documents. Julius

Wellhausen (1844–1918) brought all the threads together in what became known as the Documentary Theory.

Scholars had noticed that in some places in the Genesis text, for example, God is referred to as Elohim, and in other narratives, as Yahveh. In Hebrew, Yahveh is rendered with the letters Yod, Hey, Vav, Hey (the tetragrammaton), which Jews traditionally do not pronounce out loud. Instead they say "Adonai," meaning the Lord. On the basis of these and other differing usages, scholars began to refer to E-texts (for passages that used Elohim) and J-texts (from *Jahweh*, the German for Yahveh, for passages that used Yahveh). They also noticed that different points of view are expressed in different sections of the Torah. For example, in some places, the views of the high priests are the dominant ones, urging people to come to the Temple in Jerusalem, to bring sacrifices in abundance, and to observe the various rituals described in detail. Scholars labeled these P-texts (for Priestly). The P-texts are largely found in the books of Leviticus and Numbers.

The Documentary Theory argues that there was an editor who added to and stitched all of these different texts together. He became known as the "redactor." These are known as R-texts.

Wellhausen's approach was not welcomed with open arms. Biblical literalists were shocked and angry. They felt that the sacredness of the Bible was being called into question.

Most non-Orthodox Jews have learned to accept and work with the Documentary Theory. Most mainline Protestants do as well, as do Catholic biblical scholars.

There is a wide range of opinions, however, about the assignment of texts within one document or another. Scholar Richard Elliot Friedman discusses the Documentary Theory with great care in his book *Who Wrote the Bible?* Friedman writes:

The sources J, E, and P were found to flow through the first four of the five Books of Moses: Genesis, Exodus, Leviticus, and Numbers. However, there was hardly a trace of them in the fifth book, Deuteronomy, except for a few lines in the last chapters. Deuteronomy is written in an entirely different style from those of the other four books. The differences are obvious even in translation. The vocabulary is different. There are different recurring expressions and favorite phrases. There are doublets of whole sections of the first four books. There are blatant contradictions of detail between it and the others. Even part of the wording of the Ten Commandments is different. Deuteronomy appeared to be independent, a fourth source. It was called D.[1]

These texts seem to have an almost anti-Temple point of view; their emphasis is prophetic rather than ritualistic.

Much of the Christian world has embraced such critical understandings of the Bible's origins while still affirming its value and sacredness in religious and spiritual life. Others, however, remain inalterably opposed to the Documentary Theory. While many Orthodox and Modern Orthodox Jews do not accept it either, they acknowledge that there are textual problems within the Bible. Modern Orthodox Jews follow the intellectual and religious leadership of Yeshiva University in New York. Noah Feldman, a professor at Harvard Law School, who grew up in a Modern Orthodox family and attended a Modern Orthodox day school, wrote this in an article in the *New York Times Magazine*.

I can recall the agonies suffered by my head of school when he stopped by our biology class to discuss the problem of creation. Following the best modern Orthodox doctrine, he pointed out that Genesis could be understood allegorically, and that the length of a day might be numbered in billions of years considering that the sun, by which our time is reckoned, was not created until the fourth such "day." Not for him the embarrassing claim, heard sometimes among the ultra-Orthodox, that dinosaur fossils were embedded by God within the earth at the moment of creation in order to test our faith in biblical inerrancy. Natural selection was for him a scientific fact to be respected like the laws of physics—guided by God but effectuated though the workings of the natural order. Yet even he could not leave the classroom without a final caveat. "The truth is," he said, "despite what I have just told you, I still have a hard time believing that man could be descended from monkeys."[2]

Not oblivious to the difficulties of the biblical text, rabbinic commentaries, along with comments on individual passages found in the Talmud and its rabbinic commentaries, dealt with the texts in many ways.

There were even passages that the rabbis did not like. The principle of *lex talionis* (Latin for the "law of retaliation") is a prime example. Its classic expression is found in Exodus 21:23–25: "If any harm follows, then you shall give life for life, eye for eye, tooth for tooth, hand for hand, foot for foot, burn for burn, wound for wound, stripe for stripe."

In the Sermon on the Mount, Matthew quotes Jesus as saying "You have heard that it was said, 'An eye for an eye and a tooth for a tooth.' But I say to you, Do not resist an evil-doer. But if anyone strikes you on the right cheek, turn the other also" (Matthew 5:38–39). Through the ages, Christians have interpreted Jesus's words as an implicit criticism of Judaism as a religion of vengeance.

But that is hardly a fair characterization. Even at its most literal level, without rabbinic interpretation, this verse conveys the meaning that one should not extract a greater payment than the one suffered. But the rabbis went further. They understood that the plain meaning of the text was rarely put into practice and argue that the recompense for an eye was likely to be a monetary payment of a value equivalent to the loss.

Aspersions by church fathers on the teachings of Judaism found in the Bible were designed to "prove" that Christianity was superior to Judaism. But the rabbis were humane and compassionate in their deliberations. Historically, most church teachers had little if any access to or interest in rabbinic commentaries.

And we must keep in mind and insist upon distinguishing the religion of Judaism from the religion of the Old Testament. Judaism is not identical with Old Testament religion. This fact, which Christian theologians persistently refuse to acknowledge, has been known and accepted by every professing rabbinic Jew ever since the doctrine of the authority of the traditional law has been proclaimed, which was a long time before Christianity came into the world. The Old Testament contains simply the foundation of Judaism but the superstructure is larger than the foundation. Furthermore, the Old Testament, besides containing the principles upon which Judaism is built, also, especially in the Pentateuch, the constitution and the civil and criminal codes of law, are intended for the ancient Kingdoms of Judah and Israel. And whether some of these laws, found in this statute book of ancient Jewish states, can meet with the approval of modern conceptions of just and humane state laws or not; whether they compare favorably or unfavorably with the laws on the statute books of modern civilized states, discriminating in their legislation between their own citizens and those of other countries, these are questions with which we are not now concerned. What concerns us in our present discussion is the fact that the laws for the ancient Jewish state, like so many other laws found in the Pentateuch, do not form part of the Jewish religion as such.

Jacob Z. Lauterbach, "Jew and Non-Jew,"
Central Conference of American Rabbis Yearbook
1921, p. 163

SLAVERY

On certain issues, some Christian traditions have historically selected verses from the Bible that support its positions, while ignoring or dismissing those that call them into question. An excellent example has to do with the institution of slavery in the United States.

The Southern Baptist Convention represents more than sixteen million Americans, second only to the Roman Catholic Church, which has nearly 70 million members in the United States. Like many religious groups in America, the Civil War and slavery were major factors in its development.

Let's look at some of the biblically based arguments for and against slavery used in the Civil War period. In 1841, slavery apologist Thornton Stringfellow wrote: "In Genesis God punished Ham's transgressions with 'cursed be Canaan ... a servant of servants shall he be to his brethren.'"[3] Africans, he said, are the descendants of Ham and thus destined to serve the descendants of Shem and

Japheth, "from whom have sprung the Jews and all nations of Europe and America and a great part of Asia."[4] He also pointed out that in Genesis 12, biblical patriarchs had male and female slaves.

Theodore Dwight Weld in *The Bible Against Slavery* (1837), wrote, "It is not clear that to 'serve' God means chattel-slavery. It is not at all clear that Africans are the descendants of Ham. Such an interpretation seems to confuse the mark of Cain (which can be interpreted as dark skin) with the curse of Canaan."[5]

Former slave Frederick Douglass was one of the foremost leaders of the abolitionist movement and an adviser to President Lincoln during the Civil War. He wrote in his *Narrative of the Life of Frederick Douglass, An American Slave* in 1845:

> It is plain that a very different-looking class of people are springing up in the south, and are now held in slavery, from those originally brought to this country from Africa; and if their increase will do no other good, it will do away the force of argument that God cursed Ham, and therefore American slavery is right. If the lineal descendants of Ham are alone to be scripturally enslaved, it is certain that slavery at best becomes unscriptural; for thousands are ushered into this world, annually, who like myself, owe their existence to white fathers, and those fathers [are] most frequently their own masters.[6]

In 1995 the Southern Baptist Convention voted to renounce its racist roots and apologize for its past defense of slavery. Indeed, it was only then that the Convention formally acknowledged that racism had played a role in its founding.

The Bible is none other than the Voice of Him that sitteth upon the Throne! Every book of it,—every Chapter of it,—every Verse of it,—every word of it,—every syllable of it,—(where are we to stop?)—every letter of it—is the direct utterance of the Most High! The Bible is none other than the word of God: not some part of it, more, some part of it, less; but all alike, the utterance of Him who sitteth upon the Throne;—absolute,—faultless,—unerring,—supreme!

Dean John William Burgon,
Essays and Reviews

BIBLICAL INERRANCY

At the heart of much conservative Christian thinking is the belief in biblical inerrancy. In the words of the faith statement adopted by the Southern Baptist Convention, "The Holy Bible was written by men divinely inspired and is God's revelation of Himself to man. It is a perfect treasure of divine instruction.... Therefore, all scripture is totally true and trustworthy."[7]

In practice, however, not every verse in the Bible is equally observed. For example, in the same chapter of the Bible that contains the frequently quoted verses on forbidden sexual unions, there is a verse that reads, "If anyone insults his father or his mother, he shall be put to death...." (Lev. 20:9). Would any of us live past our teen years if this injunction were rigorously obeyed?

A great many Christians, however, affirm a more nuanced understanding of the Bible's texts, while still upholding its central importance in the life of faith. In 1967 the United Presbyterian Church in the United States of

America (a precursor to today's Presbyterian Church (USA) denomination) adopted a newly written confession of faith, called simply "The Confession of 1967." It includes this:

> The scriptures, given under the guidance of the Holy Spirit, are nevertheless the words of men, conditioned by the language, thought forms, and literary fashions of the places and times at which they were written. They reflect views of life, history, and the cosmos which were then current. The church, therefore, has an obligation to approach the Scriptures with literary and historical understanding. As God has spoken his word in divers cultural situations, the church is confident that he will continue to speak through the Scriptures in a changing world and in every form of human culture.

This statement was made part of the constitution of the Presbyterian Church (USA) by ratification in 1967 by 90 percent of the presbyteries of the denomination. Although biblical literalists may dominate the headlines, it's important to remember they are not the last word on "Christian" understandings of the Bible.

CREATIONISM AND INTELLIGENT DESIGN

Belief in the inerrancy of the Bible has led to all sorts of conflicts with modern scientific understanding. It was an enormous intellectual achievement for the ancients who wrote the book of Genesis to set forth patterns of creation. They wanted to understand how they came to be, and the first chapters of Genesis do exactly that. These early theories of Creation have parallels in other ancient Near Eastern texts, but in the Bible they are developed to a higher intellectual and moral level.

Literalism deprives God of his ultimacy and, religiously speaking, of his majesty. It draws him down to the level of that which is not ultimate, the finite. Faith, if it takes its symbols literally, becomes idolatrous! It calls something ultimate which is less than ultimate. Faith, conscious of the symbolic character of its symbols, gives God the honor which is due him.

Abraham Joshua Heschel in *Dynamics of Faith*, p. 52

The idea that God rested from the labors of creation, and that therefore people need to rest on the seventh day is a highly sophisticated idea, expressed in poetic terms.

Through the ages, Judaism has bowed to science. As our scientific knowledge became more advanced, we no longer regarded the Bible's ventures into cosmology, biology, and physics as literally true, instead we began to emphasize the moral and ethical dimension of the early biblical folk stories. As exemplified by Moses Maimonides (who was himself a

The literary critic looking at Genesis recognized in its narrative of Creation a myth, a transcendental account that is neither history nor science. Myths are not "true" in themselves; rather, they reflect truths. The Jews who told the creation story, and the Christians and Muslims who repeated and enriched it, knew no such distinction. Scripture was not only "true," each and every word of it; it was also *inerrant*, incapable of being false. All three communities have been more than able to treat Genesis as "myth": to unpack from it the moral and spiritual "truths" found within the narrative.

F. E. Peters, *The Voice, the Word, the Books*, p. 8

physician) in the twelfth century, science and Judaism have sel-
dom been in conflict. In fact, just the opposite was the case.
Thus, Jews have been largely absent from the raucous debate
about Charles Darwin and evolution, which seems to convulse
fundamentalist Christian theology. We regard the Bible as a
revered document of religious truth, not as a science textbook.
Similarly, many Christian traditions and many individual
Christians do not find the theory of evolution to conflict with
their interpretation of the Bible.

S ome contemporary commentators—most notably
Abraham Joshua Heschel—argue that the Bible itself
is midrash. Heschel regards the central event of biblical
theology—the revelation at Sinai—as a midrash about how
the law was given to the people of Israel. To take the narrative literally and believe that God actually spoke and
handed over tablets is, Heschel argues, to confuse metaphor
with fact. According to this view, there is only midrash, followed by midrash upon midrash. The stories of the Bible
translate God's unknowable actions into familiar human
terms that a reader can understand.

Alan Dershowitz, *The Genesis of Justice, p. 17*

Jews have looked to the Bible for inspiration, moral and
ethical guidance, and understanding about how people lived in
biblical times. Mainstream Jewish tradition has never privileged
the literal words of the Bible to the point that all other human
and scientific evidence must be cast out. Nor have the majority of Christians. Such Jews and Christians alike revere the
Bible and its words, but we read them through the constantly
evolving understanding of our great teachers and preachers.

6

ARE WE STILL WAITING FOR THE MESSIAH?

IS JESUS THE MESSIAH? Or is it Rabbi Menachem Mendel Schneerson, the late leader of the Lubavitch sect? Or maybe it was Shabbetai Tzvi, the self-proclaimed Jewish Messiah of the seventeenth century? What's a Messiah (or messiah) supposed to do anyway? To write anything about the Messiah is very difficult and confusing.

It doesn't help that popular culture often purveys a vision of Jesus that doesn't reflect a considered systematic theology and that often isn't even biblically based. And then there are the so-called predictions of the coming of Jesus the Messiah in the Hebrew Bible. Many cause confusing interpretations, particularly because some strands of Christian teaching allow for highly personalized interpretations of Scripture without reference to historical-critical methods of interpretation. Even among the majority of Christian traditions that do affirm a more nuanced approach to the Bible, concensus can be hard to reach. Even scholars differ widely on the

> One should not entertain the notion that in the Era of the Moshiah any element of the natural order will be nullified, or that there will be any innovation in the work of Creation. Rather, the world will continue according to its pattern.
>
> Maimonides, "The Messiah"

origins of messianism in the Hebrew Bible and how it developed and grew, or did not grow, in the literature of the rabbis. The increasingly influential idea of a messianic age, rather than the Messiah as a person, further confuses the nonscholarly reader. What are the origins of this idea, and why did it appear?

There is a history of false messiahs in Judaism, perhaps most infamously Shabbetai Tzvi, who declared himself in Gaza in the seventeenth century and stirred up hysteria all over the world, and then, shockingly, under threat of death from the Islamic authorities, converted to Islam. These false messiahs usually emerged at times of great oppression and loss of hope for Jews; they promised to miraculously restore the vitality of the Jewish people. Some Hasidic Jews, members of the Chabad-Lubavitch sect, have asserted that their late leader, Rabbi Menachem Mendel Schneerson, who died in 1994, is the messiah. Is Schneerson a false messiah, in the tradition of Shabbetai Tzvi?

And then there is the matter of those who claim to be Messianic Jews. That is, they claim to be Jews, but assert that Jesus is their Messiah.

We will try to examine all of these ideas to help you make sense of the term *Messiah*.

AMERICAN MESSIAHS

One of the characteristics of American religious life, especially in Protestantism, has been its private entrepreneurship. There is an American pattern of small splinter groups separating from mainline Protestant denominations. That is how the Church of Christ, the Assemblies of God, and the Jehovah's Witnesses came to be. That pattern continues today, especially among the evangelical and Pentecostal groupings. Mainline Protestant churches (Episcopal, Methodist, Lutheran, and the rest) have all experienced reductions in their memberships and church attendance, while the splinter groups have gained.

And it is from their ranks that the loudest, most emotional, and least thoughtful preachers are emerging. Many of them deliver their messianic message—that the end times are nigh—from electronic pulpits. They are rarely bound by systematic theology, biblical scholarship, or appeal to creedal statements. They seem to have instinctively understood that most people are reluctant to change. Therefore, the essential message they deliver is that Jesus approved of life as it was in some former time, often portrayed as a kind of golden age, and that he does not approve of change. They validate this antimodernist stance by taking verses out of context and using them as they wish. Their list of "antis" includes globalism, the North American Free Trade Agreement, gay marriage, abortion rights, sex education, and science teaching, among others.

Some of these Protestant preachers are not formally educated, but heard the "call to preach God's Word." This is a reflection of fundamentalism's disdain for formal education. Many of them are Pentecostal as well. The term *Pentecostalism* is derived from a Christian understanding of the biblical festival of Shavuot (Pentecost is the Christian name, also denoting fifty days), which comes seven weeks after Passover. For Jews, Shavuot marks the anniversary of the giving of the Ten Commandments. For Christians, even in mainstream churches, it marks the descent of the Holy Spirit on the people. Pentecostals speak in tongues, usually in some altered state. This, for them, is a sign that they have been baptized by the Holy Spirit.

There are certainly mystical elements in Judaism that lean in the same anti-intellectual direction as these Christian tendencies.

PROOF TEXTING

After the destruction of the Temple, in the year 70, and the beginning of the exile of Jews from the Land of Israel, two new religions emerged from that biblical foundation.

Neither the rabbis nor the early Christians thought of their faith as a new religion, although in both cases, it really was. The church fathers, however, understood that they were developing a new religion. Therefore, they sought justification for their new beliefs and practices by appealing to biblical proof texts.

University of Miami professor of religious studies William Scott Green, in his essay "Messiah in Judaism," in *Judaisms and their Messiahs at the Turn of the Christian Era*, points out that

> any notion of a messianic belief or idea in ancient Judaism necessarily pre-supposes that "messiah" was a focal and evocative native category for ancient Jews. But a review of Israelite and early Judaic literature, the textual record produced and initially preserved by Jews, makes such a conclusion dubious at best. The noun *mashiah* (anointed or anointed one) occurs 38 times in the Hebrew Bible, where it applies twice to the patriarchs, six times to the high priest, once to Cyrus, and 29 times to the Israelite king, primarily Saul and secondarily David or an unnamed Davidic monarch. In these contexts the term denotes one invested, usually by God, with power and leadership, but never an eschatological figure. Ironically, in the apocalyptic book of Daniel (9:25*ff.*), where an eschatological messiah would be appropriate, the term refers to a murdered high priest.[1]

New Testament authors, especially Matthew and Luke, saw in the Hebrew Bible "promise-fulfillment" texts describing Jesus, where, Jews believe, no such intent existed. For example, describing Jesus's early childhood flight to Egypt with his parents, Matthew writes, "And so was fulfilled what the Lord had said through the prophet: 'Out of Egypt I called my son'" (Matt. 2:15) and similar lines. This was designed to give authority to teaching as being in continuity with the religion of the Bible.

One of the most famous Christian uses of biblical text is from Isaiah 7:14: "Therefore the Lord himself will give you a sign. Look, the young woman is with child and shall bear a son, and shall name him Immanuel." The writer of Matthew's Gospel quotes from the Septuagint (Greek) version of the Isaiah text and identifies the young woman as "a virgin." However, the original Hebrew word in question is *almah*—which means "young woman." Therefore, the Jewish view is that the original Hebrew text is not predicting the virgin birth.

FALSE MESSIAHS

One of the Jewish responses to times of persecution has been to hope for a redeemer, a figure raised by God, who, through some magical or divine intervention, would end all of their problems. Certainly, the oppressive Roman regime in first-century Israel was among the most heinous in history. The Romans were quite apprehensive about charismatic figures who might rally the people to resist the procurators' iron fist. Jesus was, for some, just such a figure.

Bar Kochba was the key figure in one of the most widely storied revolts against the Romans in 135 CE. Jews flocked to him as their new leader, and he was widely perceived as a messiah. The Romans sent massive forces to defeat him. It is not known how Bar Kochba died, but he was widely perceived as a messiah.

Other false messiahs followed him. In eighth-century Persia, Abu Isa al-Isfahani claimed to be the precursor of the messiah. We have already mentioned the notorious Kabbalist Shabbetai Tzvi. In the eighteenth century, Jewish religious leader Jacob Frank claimed to be the reincarnation of King David.

One of the most curious occurrences of modern Jewish history is the advent of a group of Hasidic Jews who are part of the Chabad-Lubavitch sect, headquartered in Crown Heights, Brooklyn, which was led for many years by Rabbi Menachem Mendel Schneerson. Schneerson developed this group into a worldwide movement promoting ultra-Orthodox Judaism. During the last years of his life and after his death in 1994, many began to think of him as the Messiah.

With the challenge of Zionism, much Hasidic discussion of eschatology has focused on the nature of historical redemption. The interpretation of the well-known talmudic statement according to which Jews vowed not to rebel against the nations, implying a prohibition of political independence prior to the Messiah's advent, has, for example, taken on central importance, as has an occasional tendency to demonize Zionism as a metaphysical evil rather than an halakhic error. This position is most vigorously urged by certain Hungarian writers, most notably the late Satmarer Rebbe, R. Yoel Teitelbaum.

Contemporary events have also precipitated a change in the traditional outlook of Habad Hasidism. Traditionally, this school avoided explicit messianic speculation. In recent years, however, the late Lubavitcher Rebbe and his followers have preached the imminence of

the messianic era. This emphasis is perhaps not uncon-
nected to their position on the State of Israel, which com-
bines a rejection of the Zionist movement with a hard line
on the retention of territory taken in the Six-Day War and
even in the various incursions into Lebanon.

Norman Lamm, *The Religious Thought of*
Hasidism, p. 516

THE MESSIANIC AGE

The advent of an era of peace and harmony, which was to be
heralded by the Messiah, is a notion that has an important place
in Jewish thinking. The issue at hand, however, is whether this
era will come about through an external force imposing it upon
people, through the conscious, deliberate efforts of human
beings, or through some combination of the two.

With the Enlightenment, there were dramatic changes
in the legal and social position of the Jews and the way in
which they, in turn, looked upon the world in which they
lived. The French Revolution in 1789, stimulated by the
rationalism of the Enlightenment and the success of the
American Revolution in 1776, brought still more significant
changes. Reform Judaism began as a lay movement in
Germany in 1810 through the leadership of Israel Jacobson.
The worship service was shortened; the chaotic appearance
of the Orthodox prayer service was replaced by a Protestant-
like orderly service; men and women sat together; sermons
were preached in German; the organ was introduced into the
synagogue. Firmly rooted in eighteenth-century rationalism,
the Reform movement specifically discarded the notion that
some anointed individual would appear to cure all the woes of
humanity. The messianic age was understood as the ultimate

triumph of enlightened humanism, not as a supernatural event.

For some early Zionists, the advent of a modern Jewish state in 1948 was a sign of the coming of the messianic age. But in the early years after Israel was founded, many Orthodox Jews protested that only the Messiah could establish a Jewish state in ancient Palestine and opposed the Zionist idea. Most of them, with a few exceptions (the Neturei Karta and Satmar Hasidim), have now accepted the existence of the State of Israel.

MESSIANIC JEWS

Messianic Judaism, as we know it today, is the heir to the late nineteenth-century Hebrew Christian movement. Hebrew Christians, and today's Messianic Jews (the best-known group of which styles itself Jews for Jesus) believe that Jesus completes Judaism, and that only those Jews who accept Jesus as the Messiah are authentically Jewish. This movement is more romantic in its understanding of Judaism than it is factually correct in its practice.

Those who support the Jewish identity of Hebrew Christians are usually among those Jews who believe that anyone who wishes to call himself or herself Jewish is Jewish. Others have a more stringent view of Jewish identity and believe that there are essential characteristics about Jewishness, all of which must be affirmed.

Messianic Jews refer to Jesus as Yeshua. They believe that God became flesh in Jesus. This concept of the corporeality of God is a major departure from the essential theological thrust of Judaism.

Messianic Judaism asserts that Jesus did not intend to start a new religion, but that the rabbis decided to separate themselves from biblical Judaism, which predicted the messiahship of Jesus.

In fact, Messianic Judaism is part of a concerted effort to convert Jews to Christianity and receives significant support from the Southern Baptist Convention, which has long held the view that for Jesus to return, the Jews must convert to Christianity. This is connected to the fundamentalist view of end times (see the chapter "End Times" for more about this idea).

Messianic synagogues frequently have Hebrew names, such as Beth Yeshua or B'nai Moshiach. Their spiritual leaders call themselves rabbis, and their worship services contain certain Jewish elements. But for the most part, their services bear a greater resemblance to what you'd experience in a fundamentalist or evangelical church than in a synagogue.

There are many different reasons people join messianic congregations. Some might believe that they are authentically Jewish and are practicing an authentic form of Judaism. Others might be angry at their childhood experiences with Judaism, and accepting Jesus might be a way of "acting out." Others may be in an interfaith marriage where a messianic synagogue represents a compromise.

However, several things are clear. Messianic synagogues are focused on converting Jews, in fulfillment of fundamentalist end-time notions. The Second Coming, these fundamentalists

What is our core identity as Jewish believers in Jesus? Most Jewish followers of y'shua have given the same answer as our Gentile counterparts through the ages: first and foremost, we are "in Christ," "in Messiah," and therefore members of his body.

"Havurah," a publication of Jews for Jesus

85

believe, will be postponed until a critical number of Jews become believers in Christianity. This also is the theological basis on which Christian Zionism is based. Messianic Judaism is about one, minority view of Christianity, not Judaism. The Hebrew Christian view of the essential sinfulness of all people, and the necessity for vicarious atonement through Jesus for entrance into the afterlife, simply removes them from normative Judaism. Cosmetic Hebraisms and Jewish-sounding phases do not make one authentically Jewish.

7

DO CHRISTIANS STILL WANT TO CONVERT US?

FOR CENTURIES, one of the great obsessions of the Christian religion has been the conversion of the Jews.

Why?

Christianity's primary goal is salvation. Many, but by no means all, Christians regard themselves as performing a great favor to Jews when they encourage them to become Christians, historically even by force. Judaism has never focused on personal salvation, therefore most Jews don't regard it as an issue. In Jewish theology, according to Kaufmann Kohler in *Jewish Theology*, there is "no salvation in Judaism by faith alone or in the mere acceptance of a creed."[1] Salvation is available to all. This same sentiment could be found in many Christian churches, too.

For some other Christians, however, the existence of an ancient people who do not accept the divinity of Jesus challenges their own belief system. It is characteristic of "daughter religions" that they regard themselves as replacements for the earlier religion. Theologians call this supersessionism.

The reason that proselytization and conversion remain issues for both Jews and Christians is that truth is not relative, and thus the ultimate truth claims of Judaism and Christianity are not only different but mutually exclusive. The highest form of worship of the Lord God of Israel is *either* by the Torah and the tradition of the Jewish people *or* by Christ and the tradition of the church. That the choice is framed in just this way is the result of the historical origins of Judaism and Christianity: both traditions originate in the history of Israel presented in the Hebrew Bible. Accordingly, our differences are over the same God who first appeared in the same story. One cannot live as a Jew and as a Christian simultaneously. One could well say that the greatest temptation for a Jew is Christianity and that the greatest temptation for a Christian is Judaism.

> David Novak, "Introduction: What to Seek and What to Avoid in Jewish-Christian Dialogue,"
> *Christianity in Jewish Terms*, p. 5

Most societies throughout history have been fairly intolerant of "the Other." In essence, people who do not conform to the majority in their looks, behavior, or beliefs are either shunned or encouraged/forced to become members of the majority. Our own world today, while fairly accepting of differences, still has its prejudices against those who do not conform to the societal norm. This might include gay men and women, atheists, and new immigrants.

Conversion was not always an ever-present and preeminent theme in Jewish-Christian relations. In many societies, Jews and Christians coexisted with mutual respect. This was certainly true in many parts of Europe during the last five hundred years. In some cases, the interdependence and mutuality of Jews and Christians was quite intense and fruitful. As Jonathan Elukin, associate professor of history at Trinity College (Hartford, Connecticut) points out in his book *Living Together, Living Apart*, the history of interaction between Jews and Christians waxed and waned through the centuries. It is not a long story of hostility, but of centuries of Jews and Christians living cooperatively side by side most of the time.

A Sea Change in the Catholic Church

The impact of World War II was enormous. Most people were stunned by the revelation that six million Jews and millions of other vulnerable minorities—gypsies, homosexuals, the mentally ill—were killed by the Nazis. People began to look at their world in a new way. Authoritarian leaders, people realized, posed a threat.

The Roman Catholic Church was not immune to this new wave of democratic thinking that was sweeping Europe and the rest of the world. Pope John XXIII called the Second Vatican Council in 1962. Those meetings in Rome, which ended in 1965, caused a profound, historic change in the Christian view of Judaism. The impact of the decisions made by the bishops and other leaders of the Church is still being felt. Some of the changes had to do with internal Church matters, others dealt with the church's relationships with the world.

The Mass is the main event of the week in most Catholic churches, and it was the Mass, the service of worship, that was most visibly altered. Until Vatican II, worshipers were essentially observers. The Mass was said or sung in Latin, and the priest and congregation faced in the same direction. After Vatican II, the local language often became the language of the Mass, either reducing or eliminating Latin altogether, and the priest faced the congregation and involved it in new ways. The exclusive use of Latin at Mass became rare, except at papal Masses in Rome.

In July 2007, Pope Benedict XVI announced that a wider permission would be given to priests to celebrate the Latin Mass as it was in the rites of 1962, before the liturgical reforms of the Second Vatican Council. While many traditionalist

Catholics were very pleased to be able to have Mass "in the old rite," it nevertheless raised concerns in the Jewish community, since the Good Friday prayer for Jews from 1962 contained language which portrayed Jews negatively. That Good Friday prayer asked that God "lift the veil covering" Jewish hearts, so that they could recognize "Jesus Christ Our Lord." Some Jewish leaders were very vocal in expressing their dismay at the wider use of these prayers, since the reformed prayers from 1970 contained only positive expressions of Jews and their relationship to the irrevocable covenant God had given them.

But it should be noted that it is doubtful that the Latin Mass will be readopted by most churches, not least because it no longer reflects the thinking of the twenty-first-century Church. *Nostra Aetate*, Vatican II's important declaration about the Church's relations with non-Catholics, fully acknowledged that Church leaders in the past had made anti-Semitic statements and engaged in anti-Semitic acts, including the assertion of deicide, blaming the Jews for killing Jesus. One of its most important statements was its revision of the assertion of Jewish deicide.

> True, the Jewish authorities and those who followed their lead pressed for the death of Christ; still, what happened in His passion cannot be charged against all the Jews, without distinction, then alive, nor against the Jews of today. Although the Church is the new people of God, the Jews should not be presented as rejected or accursed by God, as if this followed from the Holy Scriptures. All should see to it, then, that in catechetical work or in the preaching of the word of God they do not teach anything that does not conform to the truth of the Gospel and the spirit of Christ. Furthermore, in her rejection of every persecution against any man, the Church, mindful of the

patrimony she shares with the Jews and moved not by political reasons but by the Gospel's spiritual love, decries hatred, persecutions, displays of anti-Semitism, directed against Jews at any time and by anyone.[2]

In the wake of *Nostra Aetate*, there followed a series of positive acts that served further to enhance Catholic-Jewish relations. First among them is the articulation of the view that God's covenant with the Jews has not been simply replaced by a New Covenant with Christians. While this idea is accepted by most Catholics and likewise many Protestants, there remains the lingering question as to whether the Jewish covenant is sufficient for salvation in Christian terms. Since salvation in this sense is not a Jewish concern, for Jews this question is largely academic.

Greek philosophy, mediated through Islam, had influenced a segment of Iberian Jewry to think in universal and rational terms to the point where the particular rituals and even beliefs of Judaism seemed of little consequence. When the situation of Spanish Jewry deteriorated in the late fourteenth century and Jews in various communities were offered the Cross or the sword in 1391, many Spanish Jews chose Christianity. Others converted, without extreme coercion, during the following century. They could, after all, be Aristotelians in Christian garb as well as in Jewish. Some remained secretly Jewish, but even these were ready to pretend they were Christians in order to save their lives. Spanish Jewry thus foreshadows the modern period, a time when identification with non-Jewish values leaves Jewishness—and not just Jews—vulnerable to anti-Semitism.

Michael Meyer, *Jewish Identity in the Modern World*, pp. 34–35

1994 CATECHISM

The *Catechism of the Catholic Church* contains the essential teachings of the Roman Catholic Church. In the latest edition (1994), speaking of the relationship of the Church with the Jewish people, we find the following statement:

> When she delves into her own mystery, the Church, the People of God in the New Covenant, discovers her link with the Jewish People, "the first to hear the Word of God." The Jewish faith, unlike other non-Christian religions, is already a response to God's revelation in the Old Covenant. To the Jews "belong the sonship, the glory, the covenants, the giving of the law, the worship and the promises; to them belong the patriarchs, and of their race, according to the flesh, is the Christ," "for the gifts and the call of God are irrevocable."[3]

With the affirmation of the Jewish Covenant came statements that Catholics should not target Jews for conversion. The United States Conference of Catholic Bishops, through its many committees and commissions, has affirmed, promoted, and institutionalized this new relationship with the Jewish community. Pope John Paul II was the first pope to make an official papal visit to a synagogue, when he visited Rome's main synagogue in 1986; he also visited Israel in 2000. Needless to say, there are areas in which Jews and Catholics still do not agree. This is particularly so in relation to the Holocaust and the role of the Church during the Nazi reign.

While there may not be agreement on every issue, there exists now a sense of mutual respect and collegiality between the Roman Catholic Church and the Jewish community, particularly in America.

American Protestants

Similar changes have taken place in many American Protestant denominations. It is fascinating to note that even these churches, separated for centuries from Rome, have in many ways followed the Vatican in Jewish-Christian relations. They all articulate the idea that God's covenant with the Jews remains valid, alongside a second covenant through Jesus. This has been a significant step away from earlier church efforts at conversion.

In 1997, the General Convention of the Episcopal Church in the United States affirmed its desire to work with Jews and other religious groups in communities throughout America. But even before that, conversion of Jews was not a high priority for the Episcopal Church.

In statement after statement from the General Convention, the Episcopal Church has distanced itself from any effort to evangelize Jews. In many communities warm relations between synagogues and local Episcopal churches exist, and a strong commitment to interfaith work flourishes.

One of the flash points in Jewish-Presbyterian relations has been over a Messianic congregation, in the outskirts of Philadelphia, designed to evangelize Jews. Funding for this church came from the national Presbyterian Church as well as from the local synod in Philadelphia and Pennsylvania. The national church ultimately defunded this project, but not before relations between the Jewish community and the Presbyterian Church became frayed.

On April 18, 1994, the Evangelical Lutheran Church in America, the largest Lutheran body in the United States, issued the following statement.

In the long history of Christianity there exists no more tragic development than the treatment accorded the Jewish people on the part of Christian believers. Very few Christian communities of faith were able to escape the contagion of anti-Judaism and its modern successor, anti-Semitism. Lutherans belonging to the Lutheran World Federation and the Evangelical Lutheran Church in America feel a special burden in this regard because of certain elements in the legacy of the reformer Martin Luther and the catastrophes, including the Holocaust of the twentieth century, suffered by Jews in places where the Lutheran churches were strongly represented.

The Lutheran communion of faith is linked by name and heritage to the memory of Martin Luther, teacher and reformer. Honoring his name in our own, we recall his bold stand for truth, his earthly and sublime words of wisdom, and above all his witness to God's saving Word. Luther proclaimed a gospel for people as we really are, bidding us to trust a grace sufficient to reach our deepest shames and address the most tragic truths.

In the spirit of that truth-telling, we who bear his name and heritage must with pain acknowledge also Luther's anti-Judaic diatribes and the violent recommendations of his later writings against the Jews. As did many of Luther's own companions in the sixteenth century, we reject this violent invective, and yet more do we express our deep and abiding sorrow over its tragic effects on subsequent generations. In concert with the Lutheran World Federation, we particularly deplore the appropriation of Luther's words by modern anti-Semites for the teaching of hatred toward Judaism or toward the Jewish people in our day.

> Grieving the complicity of our own tradition within this history of hatred, moreover, we express our urgent desire to live out our faith in Jesus Christ with love and respect for the Jewish people. We recognize in anti-Semitism a contradiction and an affront to the Gospel, a violation of our hope and calling, and we pledge this church to oppose the deadly working of such bigotry, both within our own circles and in the society around us. Finally, we pray for the continued blessing of the Blessed One upon the increasing cooperation and understanding between Lutheran Christians and the Jewish community.[4]

This forthright statement from the more liberal of the two Lutheran churches in America tells the entire story. The more conservative Missouri Synod is only minimally engaged in interfaith work.

The Methodist Church has its origins in eighteenth-century England. Its founders were John Wesley and his brother Charles. In 1996, and readopted in 2004, the United Methodist Church promulgated a position paper entitled "Building New Bridges in Hope." This extraordinary document, drawing on earlier Church statements, affirms that

> Christians and Jews are bound to God through biblical covenants that are eternally valid. As Christians, we stand firm in our belief that Jesus was sent by God as the Christ to redeem all peoples, and that in Christ the biblical covenant has been made radically new. While church tradition has taught that Judaism has been superseded by Christianity and the 'new Israel,' we do not believe that earlier covenantal relationships have been invalidated or that God has abandoned Jewish partners in the covenant.[5]

The Church has clearly expressed its desire to enter into conversations to build relationships with the Jewish community. "We dare to believe that such conversations and acts will build new bridges in hope between Christians and Jews, and that they will be among the signs and the first fruits of our sibling relationship under our parent God. Together, we await and strive for the fulfillment of God's reign."[6]

The Southern Baptists are the largest Protestant denomination in the United States and the most indigenously American.

The theology of the Southern Baptists runs parallel to most of the fundamentalist and evangelical groups described in the chapter "End Times." It is also intimately tied to the Christian Zionist movement. Converting Jews has long been an important part of the theology of the Southern Baptist Convention.

Jewish organizations have generally stated that the drive for conversion is disrespectful and violates the American notion of religious tolerance. But there is more at stake here. It's about much more than mere courtesy.

The Southern Baptists seek to delegitimize the Jewish experience throughout history, seeing Judaism as merely a prelude to the beginnings of Christianity. Replacement theology, as this is called, is central to Southern Baptist thinking, and relates closely to its attitudes toward other non-Christians.

A key Bible verse that motivates evangelical Christians to emphasize the conversion of the Jews is from John 14:6: "I am the way, and the truth, and the life. No one comes to the Father except through me." This verse serves to validate missionary activities aimed at Jews and other non-Christians, cancels out the Jewish biblical experience with God, and places Judaism merely as a prelude to the New Covenant that God made with Christ and his Church. This understanding also renders inauthentic every other religion in the world.

Jews seem to have been an obsession with Southern Baptists since 1867, when the first resolution to convert Jews was adopted. In 1987, former Southern Baptist Convention president Reverend Bailey Smith, of Dallas, said publicly that God does not hear the prayers of Jews. This assertion was later repeated in 1994, when he said, "With all due respect to those dear people, … God does not hear the prayer of a Jew."[7]

While the Southern Baptist Convention has been one of the main supporters of various manifestations of Messianic Judaism (see chapter 6, "Are We Still Waiting for the Messiah?") the Convention itself criticized "an organized effort on the part of some either to deny that the Jewish people need to come to their Messiah, Jesus, to be saved, or to claim, for whatever reason, Christians have neither the right nor obligation to proclaim the gospel to Jewish people."[8] This is a direct reference to the Roman Catholic Church (and similarly to all Christians working toward improved Jewish-Christian relations), which stated that the Jewish covenant with God is still in effect and valid.

Indeed, the matter can be summarized by quoting Dr. R. Albert Mohler, Jr., president of the Louisville Southern Baptist Theological Seminary, when he said that "we have no right to exclude Jewish persons from the promise of the Gospel."[9]

The Church of Jesus Christ of Latter-day Saints (Mormons) differs in many matters of doctrine and practice from Protestantism. Mormons don't believe in original sin or the Trinity. They are ardent missionaries, however. One of the most interesting aspects of the behavior of Latter-day Saints (LDS) toward Jews is the posthumous baptisms of several hundred thousand Jews who died in the Holocaust, in an effort to assist them in the afterlife. Jewish organizations have strenuously objected to this practice because it reminds them of eras when Jews were forcibly baptized. The LDS Church, in an agreement with an organization of Holocaust survivors, acknowledged that the practice of baptizing Jews after their deaths was offensive and issued a directive to its members to cease the practice.

Whether the efforts of some Christians to convert Jews will be effective or not remains to be seen, but one thing is clear. The conversion of the Jews has lost its great impetus in most of contemporary Christianity, particularly in the United States. Indeed, in many scholarly circles, the affirmation of the Jewishness of Jesus has become an important and affirmative theme of church teaching.

Based on many actions already taken by many churches, we can look forward to a better understanding of Jews and Judaism by most Christian denominations. And we can anticipate a more measured approach to conversion, even by its most ardent advocates.

8

ISRAEL AND THE CHRISTIANS

ISRAEL FIGURES VERY PROMINENTLY in the theology of evangelical Christianity, as well as in its attitudes toward U.S. foreign policy. Some leaders in the American and Israeli Jewish communities regard Christian Zionism and Jewish Zionism as the same thing. While there certainly are many similarities, there are vast historical and theological differences between the two.

As Walter Laqueur makes very clear in *A History of Zionism,* "The emergence of Zionism in the 1880s and 1890s can be understood only against the general background of European and Jewish history since the French Revolution on the one hand, and the spread of modern anti-Semitism on the other."[1]

Stimulated by the Enlightenment and the philosophies of Locke, Hume, Voltaire, and Rousseau, and galvanized by the forces unleashed by the French and American revolutions, the intellectual and political landscape of Europe was beyond recognition in the late eighteenth and early nineteenth centuries. The ghetto walls of Europe began to fall. The emancipation of the Jews had begun when Moses Mendelssohn, the German Jewish thinker and communal leader, rose in prominence in the 1750s. Laqueur notes, "What gave Moses Mendelssohn his importance was not that he was a great philosopher, major essayist or revolutionary theologian. His philosophical writings were quickly forgotten and his attempts to prove the existence of God were neither original nor did they have a lasting impact. His main achievement was to show, by his own example, that despite all adversity a Jew could have a thorough knowledge of modern culture and converse on equal terms with the shining lights of contemporary Europe."[2]

When the first Zionist congress met in Basel in 1897 there was no mention of Socialism. Most of those present would have angrily rejected any attempt to adulterate Zionism with Socialist ideas. But only a few years later Zionist-Socialist parties had become an integral part of the movement for a Jewish national renaissance, and within a little more than three decades Labor Zionism emerged as the strongest political force. Its growth and the impact of its ideas were of decisive importance, for it shaped the character of the Zionism movement, and subsequently the State of Israel, to a greater extent than any other group.

Walter Laqueur, *A History of Zionism*, p. 270

As Jews emerged from the ghettos of central Europe, they began to take part in its cultural, business, and intellectual life, particularly in Germany. Since almost all of religious Judaism in this period was very narrowly Orthodox, it had little to say to these newly emerging modern people. There were clear declarations of alienation from Judaism and large-scale conversions to Christianity. Mendelssohn's own children converted, as did many others. It was said that half the Jews in Berlin converted, but this was clearly an exaggeration. Laqueur notes that "it was a conflict between modern philosophy and a moribund religion."[3]

One response to modernity in the very early days of the nineteenth century in Germany was Reform Judaism. Despite the disdain of many in the Orthodox community, Reform Judaism took on the important role of saving Jews for Judaism. Services were shortened, the chaotic appearance of the Orthodox prayer service was replaced by a Protestant-like orderly service, men and women sat together, and the main language of prayer was changed from Hebrew, which few people understood, to German. The organ was introduced into the synagogues (now called temples) and the music was provided by a mixed choir of both men and women. The bar mitzvah was eliminated for the boys, and a new ceremony called confirmation (borrowed from the Lutherans) was introduced for both boys and girls. References to a "return to Zion" were eliminated from the prayerbooks. These Jews no longer felt like exiles; they embraced Germany as their homeland with Judaism as their faith, not their identity. This sense of security was fragile, however.

The traditional hope for return to Zion could not be allowed to remain in the liturgy even as a pious dream, for its presence might call into question the unqualified loyalty of the Jew to the state. It was replaced by the doctrine of the "mission of Israel," the belief that the Jews had been dispersed in the world by a beneficent Providence to act as its teachers and its guides toward the ideals of justice and righteousness revealed in the Bible.

Arthur Hertzberg, *The Zionist Idea*, p. 23

The failure of the liberal revolutions of 1848 in Germany encouraged many German Jews to emigrate to the

United States. There also was an increase in anti-Semitism during this period, as there was in 1870, when Jewish bankers were blamed for the financial crisis.

For Eastern Europe, the Enlightenment came almost a century later, and it manifested itself in a different way. While there were Jewish writers who were concerned with individual freedoms for all people, there was a general movement in the East for ethnic and nationalist freedom. This was the period in which the far-flung nationalities of the czar's empire sought land and their own national identities. This was true of the Jews as well.

> What marks modern Zionism as a fresh beginning in Jewish history is that its ultimate values derive from the general milieu. The Messiah is now identified with the dream of an age of individual liberty, national freedom, and economic social justice—i.e. with the progressive faith of the nineteenth century.
>
> Arthur Hertzberg, *The Zionist Idea*, p. 18

To escape anti-Semitism and to promote Jewish freedom, various proposals were made throughout the nineteenth century for Jewish homelands in places other than in Ottoman-ruled Palestine. For example, in 1840, Mordecai Manuel Noah proposed a Jewish nation be founded on Grand Island, near Buffalo, New York.

Theodor Herzl (1860–1904), an Austrian journalist, was a correspondent at the Paris trial of Alfred Dreyfus, a French army officer. Dreyfus had been accused of being a German spy. While he was later cleared of all charges, his military trial and conviction was the result of serious anti-Semitism in France and other parts of Europe. In his 1896 book *The Jewish State*, Herzl wrote, "the Jews have but one way of saving themselves—a return to their own people and their own land."[4] At the World Zionist Conference in Basel, Switzerland, in 1897, which Herzl organized, Britain's offer of a Jewish homeland in Uganda was rejected, but the idea of establishing an enlightened, progressive liberal Jewish state in Palestine took hold.

The new Zionist movement almost collapsed in Western Europe after Herzl's death. But in Russia the idea of a Jewish state remained a pregnant idea with little actual result. Palestine was a place to which elderly Jews went to die and be buried. Some Hasidic Jews settled there, as did a handful of Eastern European Jews fleeing the czarist and communist regimes. In the 1930s, the Jewish population of Palestine grew rapidly as European Jews fled there from Nazi persecution. Palestine also became a place of refuge for limited numbers of homeless Jews during the Second World War and its aftermath.

Zionist impulses from a generation earlier became a reality when Jewish lives needed saving; Israel, the modern Jewish state, was founded in 1948.

CHRISTIAN ZIONISM

Christian Zionism is entirely different from the Jewish Zionist movement. Its motivations have nothing to do with saving Jewish lives. The whole enterprise is ultimately about converting Jews to Christianity. Some Jewish supporters of Israel have encouraged Christian Zionism without evaluating its theological basis. Christian Zionism is directly related to dispensationalism in that its proponents believe the return of the Jews to the Promised Land is the beginning of the fulfillment of biblical prophecy.

Christian Zionism and Jewish Zionism do have one important thing in common: Both use the Promised Land verses in the Hebrew Bible to buttress their cases. "Now the Lord said to Abram, 'Go from your country and your kindred and your father's house to the land that I will show you....' Then the Lord appeared to Abram and said, 'To your offspring I will give this land'" (Genesis 12:7). These statements from the Hebrew Bible "prove" the Christian assertion that there must always be a Jewish presence in Palestine.

Christian Zionism is based on verses in the New Testament as well, especially the book of Revelation. Dispensationalism teaches that Christ will not return to reign on earth until certain events occur. Among them is the return of the Jews to the Land of Israel, the conversion to belief in Jesus, and the rapture, when, in the last days, those who are born again will be taken up into the heavens. Then the anti-Christ will reign on earth, destroying the unfaithful. Those who were saved in the rapture will then return to the Holy Land under the rule of Jesus.

Obstacle or no obstacle, it is certain the Temple will be rebuilt. Prophecy demands it.... With the Jewish nation reborn in the land of Palestine, ancient Jerusalem once again under total Jewish control for the first time in 2,100 years, and talk of rebuilding the great Temple, the most important sign of Jesus Christ's second coming is before us.... It is like the key piece of a jigsaw puzzle being found.... For all ... who trust in Jesus Christ, it is a time of electrifying excitement.

Hal Lindsey, *The Final Battle*

The third International Christian Zionist Congress, meeting in Jerusalem in 1996, stated:

God the Father, Almighty, chose the ancient nation and people of Israel, the descendants of Abraham, Isaac and Jacob, to reveal His plan of redemption for the world. They remain elect of God, and without the Jewish nation His redemptive purposes for the world will not be completed.

Jesus of Nazareth is the Messiah and has promised to return to Jerusalem, to Israel and to the world.

It is reprehensible that generations of Jewish peoples have been killed and persecuted in the name of our Lord, and we challenge the Church to repent of any sins of commission or omission against them.

The modern Ingathering of the Jewish People to *Eretz Israel* and the rebirth of the nation of Israel are in fulfillment of biblical prophecies, as written in both Old and New Testaments.

Christian believers are instructed by Scripture to acknowledge the Hebraic roots of their faith and to actively assist and participate in the plan of God for the Ingathering of the Jewish People and the Restoration of the nation of Israel in our day.[5]

While Christian Zionism is a favorite theme of evangelical Christians in the United States, its development and motivations are completely at variance with the theology and politics of Jews in many countries and the State of Israel.

Some supporters of Israel feel that Christian Zionism, despite its theology, provides important support for the State of Israel. Other Jews disagree; for example, Rabbi Eric Yoffie, president of the Union for Reform Judaism, at a June 2007 meeting of the Board of Trustees of the Union, observed that many Jewish Federations in the United States supported local dinners organized by Christians United for Israel, an organization headed by Rev. John Hagee, an evangelical pastor from San Antonio, Texas.

Yoffie said,

> For John Hagee, support for Israel is a Biblical mandate, and that mandate includes keeping every inch of occupied Arab territory. Therefore, while his dinners are supposedly non-political, in fact, that is almost never the case; instead, they advocate his hard-right political line. At a recent event in Northern Virginia, one speaker after another got up and condemned anyone who might ever consider trading "land for peace." It might be helpful to point out that the current government of Israel supports the principle of "land for peace"; and so too do most Israelis and most American Jews. Can you really say you support Israel when you attack the platform of Israel's Prime Minister and ruling coalition? And can you really say that you are helping Israel when you advocate an approach to peace that is not only opposed by Israel and American Jews, but by the Bush Administration, the Republican party, the Democratic party, and the majority of the American people?[6]

CHRISTIANITY AND U.S. FOREIGN POLICY

While liberal Christians in the United States, who are far less organized than fundamentalist Christians, generally support the existence of the State of Israel, many denominations have expressed impatience with the lack of resolution for the Israel-Palestinian conflict. They have also criticized many policies of the government of Israel vis-à-vis Palestinian refugees and repressive actions in the Palestinian territories. It needs to be said that many Israelis are just as critical of their own government on these and many other issues, and Israelis regard such criticism of their government to be a manifestation of their free and democratic society. In contrast, much of the organized American Jewish community refuses to countenance any criticism of Israeli policy.

Recalling the impact they had on hastening the fall of apartheid in South Africa, several mainline Protestant denominations have considered promoting a "phased, selective divestment in multinational corporations operating in Israel" in order to bring pressure on Israel to modify its policies toward the Palestinians. In June 2004, the Presbyterian Church (U.S.A.) voted for divestment. Stung by the criticism from the American Jewish community and fundamentalist Protestants, the resolution was modified two years later removing most of its teeth. Instead of divestment, it now called for proactively engaging with companies doing business in Israel, and it apologized for any hurt that it might have caused. Other denominations that were considering divestiture resolutions pulled back, fearing the rupture of peaceful Jewish-Christian relations in the United States.

There has been a very successful "Jewish lobby" in Washington, D.C. The principal agency is the American Israel Public Affairs Committee (AIPAC), which has been accused by some of representing only the right wing of Israel's political spectrum. AIPAC has, however, galvanized the pro-Israel sentiment in Washington.

In recent years, fundamentalist and evangelical Christians have succeeded in dominating the foreign relations forum in the United States, even though they do not represent the mainstream of Americans or Israelis. Some people argue that U.S. foreign policy in the Middle East is controlled by a conspiracy of Jews and neo-Conservatives, and believe that there is an inappropriately powerful Jewish lobby in Washington. Others, however, affirm the view of Walter

Russell Mead as stated in the September/October 2006 edition of *Foreign Affairs* in his article "God's Country?": "Evangelicals have been gaining social and political power, while liberal Christians and secular intellectuals have been losing it. This should not be blamed on the Jews."[7]

What is fascinating here is how much of an impact religious ideology is having on U.S. foreign policy. The overriding interest has not always been what's good for the United States and for the world order, or what is good for Israel, but rather what is theologically important to this one disproportionately influential segment of the American polity.

Jews need to remember that the dispensationalist theology of most evangelicals is inimical to Jews. Their views about Israel's claim to land are based on literalist interpretations of the Hebrew Bible, have much in common with the right wing of Orthodox Judaism, and have very little in common with what most Israelis believe. Literalist interpretations of biblical texts often have more to do with one's theological preconceptions and prejudices than the real meaning and spirit of scripture.

We Jews should be cognizant of the fact that while our goals seem to be the same as those of Christian Zionists—support for Israel—there might be some pitfalls along the way.

9

PROTESTANT CHURCHES TODAY: BIGGER AND SMALLER

Two SEEMINGLY CONTRADICTORY trends are operating in the world of Protestant America. The number of megachurches increases significantly each year; at the same time, small informal religious communities are also growing, and at a similar pace. We will look at these smaller, emergent churches in the next section and focus here on the megachurch phenomenon. Perhaps they are not quite as contradictory as they appear at first glance.

According to Hartford Seminary's Institute for Religion Research, in 2005 there were 1,210 Protestant churches in the United States with weekly attendance over two thousand. This was nearly double the number that existed five years previous.[1] Precise statistics for members of megachurches are hard to come by because while many of these churches do have a denominational affiliation, many do not. Yet, these megachurches represent an extraordinary trend in American religious life, and have replaced traditional mainline churches as the main religious force in America. In 2005, four megachurch pastors even had books on the *New York Times* bestseller lists.

The Hartford Institute for Religion Research has also tracked the location of megachurches. In 2005, 49 percent of these large churches were in the South, the West had 25 percent of them, and concentrations were in California, Texas, Florida, and Georgia. The number of megachurches in the

Northeast is quite small, representing perhaps 7 percent of the total.

A t its most basic descriptive level, a megachurch is a congregation which has two thousand or more worship attenders in a week. However, size alone is an insufficient characterization of this distinctive religious reality. The megachurch is a new structural and spiritual organization unlike any other. In order to understand fully the dynamics of megachurches, they must be seen as a collective social phenomenon rather than as individual anomalous moments of spectacular growth or uniquely successful entrepreneurial ventures.

Scott Thumma, "Exploring the Megachurch Phenomena: Their characteristics and cultural context," p. 1

Many reasons have been advanced to explain this major relocation in American religious life. Some analysts have suggested that the liberal influence in many of the mainline churches on hot-button issues such as abortion, homosexuality, and premarital sex has driven members to megachurches, which tend to be more conservative in their approach to current social issues. Others have suggested that the lack of a clear and consistent theology in the mainline churches is at fault.

The most probable reason for the shift in affiliation may have more to do with demographic trends in the United States. Most of the megachurches are in the suburbs: 45 percent are in newer suburbs and 29 percent are in older suburbs. People moving to the suburbs, especially to communities that are unfamiliar to them, are in need of new friendships and social relationships. While megachurches certainly have huge attendance on Sunday morning, they also offer many opportunities to study with others in small discussion groups or to serve on committees as volunteers. Most of them offer a myriad of programs for niche groups, such as families, teens, and the elderly. Perhaps the most essential need that the megachurches fulfill is providing a sense of community to people who have no community.

These churches also provide entertainment as a vibrant part of the worship experience. Most use electronic musical instruments and offer musical arrangements that are attuned to contemporary sensibilities. The words to hymns are projected onto large screens, and worship is quite accessible and involving.

Worship styles at these very large churches are continually evolving. Only 15% of churches say their format or style at any weekend service hasn't changed in the past 5 years. At the same time, almost 60% said one or more services has changed "some or a lot." This is a distinct change from our survey 5 years ago when only 42% reported a lot or some change in services. When one examines the willingness to change in those congregations that are growing most quickly, they are the churches reporting to be most likely to attempt and embrace change.

Scott Thumma, Dave Travis, Warren Bird,
"Megachurches Today 2005," p. 6

Megachurches usually are founded by dynamic preachers with charismatic personalities who bring their star power to the pulpit. It remains to be seen how many of these institutions can remain successful after the departure of their founding leaders.

Most of these large churches, while not necessarily belonging to a denomination, identify themselves as evangelical. (For further discussion of the theology of these churches, see the chapters "End Times" and "Israel and the Christians.") Their general approach to social issues and politics is quite conservative, reflecting the attitudes of the people whom they serve and the parts of the country where they are located. The conservative message found in these churches might serve as an antidote to the rapid technological and sociological changes taking place in the United States. Since many people are unnerved by these dramatic changes, they may well find a measure of comfort and familiarity in the traditional theology espoused in the megachurches.

It is also interesting to note that, according to surveys, most of these churches are far less politically active than one might think. Looking from the outside in often creates false impressions. For example, one might assume that the Roman Catholic Church is a monolith, with all of its members blindly accepting whatever dicta emerge from the curia at the Vatican. This is not the case. The Roman Catholic Church has conservatives, liberals, right-wing theologians, left-wing theologians, and every other stripe of people with varying opinions on almost every issue.

While the fundamentalist churches in America are more transparent than the Catholic Church, they too are seething with all manner of alternative opinions and views.

As Frances FritzGerald points out in her April 2007 essay "The Evangelical Surprise" in the *New York Review of Books,*

> For many Americans, the very word "evangelical" conjures
> up a vision of people railing against liberals, secularists,
> homosexuals, and the teaching of evolution in the public

schools. But such a view is inaccurate. Evangelicals are hardly identical with the Christian right, and moderate evangelical leaders have recently been making the distinction clear by publicly airing their differences with the right and challenging its positions on political issues.[2]

While it's true that fundamentalism benefited from the backlash to the excesses of the 1960s, and that the burning issues of the religious right have been abortion, same-sex marriages, and the teaching of evolution, not all American evangelicals are in lockstep with the politics of Pat Robertson or the late Jerry Falwell. In March 2007, a public rift emerged between more traditional evangelical leaders and those who wish to move the evangelical movement in a new direction. Key evangelical leaders like James C. Dobson, Gary Bauer, Tony Perkins, and Paul Weyrich wrote to the National Association of Evangelicals trying to prevent its government affairs vice president from speaking about global warming. They felt that global warming diverted attention from their traditional agenda.

However, Rev. Rick Warren, pastor of the Saddleback megachurch in Orange County, California, and author of the bestselling books *The Purpose Driven Life* and *The Purpose Driven Church*, has been urging his fellow evangelicals to broaden their agendas. He argues that there are other issues on which Christians need to focus, such as AIDS in Africa, poverty, illiteracy, and disease.

EMERGENT CHURCHES

At the opposite end of the spectrum from megachurch phenomenon is the development of small, relatively informal religious gatherings.

Almost as an underground movement, emergent churches have begun to challenge the way in which the evangelical world has done its business. These new churches have much in common with the Jewish *chavurah* movement and the Jewish Renewal movement, which trace their origins to the countercultures of the 1960s.

The *chavurah* movement came to fruition in large congregations, especially in the newer suburbs. As the American Jewish community became more structured, with its largest synagogues exposing corporate sensibilities, smaller grassroots groupings began to emerge. Among the first places in the country where *chavurah* took hold was in Southern California, in the San Fernando Valley. One large congregation had as many as fifty-eight of these small groups operating at the same time. Most were designed to help people without families nearby celebrate Jewish holidays in an intimate, communal atmosphere.

In a different vein, the Jewish Renewal movement is an outgrowth of the New Age movement. These groups, spread across the United States, are rather freeform in their liturgy, depending on atmospherics (such as candles and informal seating) as well as cross-denominational readings and prayers. Rabbi Zalman Schachter-Shalomi is the movement's spiritual father. Born in Poland in 1924 and ordained a Hasidic rabbi in America in 1947, he was struck by the seeming lack of spirituality in American Jewish life. An avid student of Jewish and non-Jewish mystical traditions, he has collaborated with the Dalai Lama, Desmond Tutu, and other prominent non-Jewish figures, and has incorporated traditionally Buddhist practices, such as meditation, into his teaching.

The emergent church movement (or conversation, as they would prefer) has many of the same characteristics of both the *chavurot* (plural of *chavurah*) and the Jewish Renewal movement, except it is within the Christian context. Their services are informal, usually in homes. Candles are lit in abundance, seating is casual, and the liturgy is relaxed. Like their Jewish counterparts, they come in for their share of criticism from their more traditional coreligionists for the unorthodoxy of their theology, its relativism, universalism, and syncretism.

Postmodern is the term that is frequently used by the emergent church leaders to describe themselves. This self-description is meant to indicate that they are deconstructing Christianity in order to reconstruct it in a way that is more appropriate for the twenty-first century. This also means looking askance at systematic theology, looking at the Bible with a more critical eye, and generally having a wider social agenda than fundamentalist or evangelical churches. One of the most prominent features of these emergent churches is their worship style. The focus is on creating an intimate and informal setting. Worship services are described as worship gatherings, with much participation, including movement, meals, and moments of personal meditation. Sermons take many different forms, sometimes as dialogues or teachings, and are often more poetic and evocative than didactic.

THE INFLUENCE OF THE CHANGES

Almost every age has seen the pendulum swing from one side of the religious spectrum to the other. The pietist Hasidic movement in Judaism grew up as a rebellion against the superlegalistic traditions of what came to be called the Mitnaged movement. American fundamentalism, as we have seen, was largely a reaction to liberal and humanist Christian theology.

In the Christian evangelical world, these emergent churches can be seen as a correction to the highly structured, corporate quality of mainline churches and the rigid politics and impersonality of the megachurches. The broadening of the social agenda will certainly cause the evangelical movement, as it is beginning to do already, to enlarge its involvement with the social welfare needs of Americans and people around the world. Emergent churches, built around small group experiences, reflect for many participants the manner in which Christianity was practiced in its earliest times.

We know from our Jewish experience with *chavurot* in the 1960s and '70s that small under-the-radar institutions can have a great impact on the established movements. Just as the social agenda and ritual practice changed and grew in Judaism as a result of the *chavurot*, the same phenomenon may occur in the mainline and megachurches. Smaller home churches can move quickly to change their focus; larger institutions may require protracted discussion that sometimes produces politically compromised resolutions, and then may require the approval of still larger bodies in order to change. It will be interesting to watch how megachurches, which seem so successful now, fare as times change, as the pendulum swings.

10

RELIGIOUS INFLUENCES ON THE
U.S. GOVERNMENT

IN CIVICS, IN U.S. HISTORY CLASSES, and in constitutional law seminars, we learned about one of the key principles of the Constitution of the United States: the separation of church and state.

This principle was derived from at least two sources: Enlightenment philosophy and the political experience of the United States' early settlers with official state churches.

Enlightenment philosophy played an important role in the philosophical underpinnings of the United States. As Mark Lilla, professor of humanities at Columbia University, wrote in his book *The Stillborn God: Religion, Politics and the Modern West*:

> Western thinkers like John Locke ... began to imagine a new kind of political order in which power would be limited, divided and widely shared; in which those in power at one moment would relinquish it peacefully at another, without fear of retribution; in which public law would govern relations among citizens and institutions; in which many different religions would be allowed to flourish, free from state interference; and in which individuals would be allowed inalienable rights to protect them from government and their fellows. This liberal-democratic order is the only one we in the West recognize as legitimate today.

117

In order to escape the destructive passions of messianic faith, political theology centered on God was replaced by political philosophy centered on man. This was the great separation.[1]

The experiences of the early settlers of the United States had made them chary of official state religions; not only the one that they experienced in England in the seventeenth and eighteenth centuries but the theocracy that the Puritans founded in Massachusetts Bay. Some of the founding fathers wrote eloquently about the separation principle. Among them were Thomas Jefferson and James Madison, who regarded the separation of religion and state as a way to protect religion against the encroachment of the state, as much as the other way around. Under the First Amendment to the Constitution of the United States, the issue is divided into two categories. First is the establishment clause: "Congress shall make no law respecting an establishment of religion, or prohibiting the free exercise thereof...." This has been interpreted over the centuries not only as a prohibition against the establishment of a national religion but against the use of tax dollars for the support of any religion at all.

The second part of the clause prohibits Congress from enacting any laws that would limit the practice of any religion. However, individual state laws have been enacted against various religious and quasireligious practices, such as bigamy, human and animal sacrifice, and the use of drugs in religious worship.

The establishment and separation clauses have been endorsed by almost every religious group in the United States, if only to prevent a rival religion from receiving the benefits of government support.

O ur challenge is different. We have made a choice that is at once simpler and harder: we have chosen to limit our politics to protecting individuals from the worst harms they can inflict on one another, to securing fundamental liberties and providing for their basic welfare, while leaving their spiritual destinies in their own hands. We have wagered that it is wiser to beware the forces unleashed by the Bible's messianic promise than to try exploiting them for the public good. We have chosen to keep our politics unilluminated by divine revelation. All we have is our own lucidity, which we must train on a world where faith still inflames the minds of men.

Mark Lilla, "The Politics of God," The New York Times Magazine, p. 55

RELIGIOUS INFLUENCES ON GOVERNMENT

Religions have not been as enthusiastic about the obverse of the establishment clause, if such an idea of reciprocity is possible. Most religions in America try to influence the government largely through lobbying efforts. Most religious denominations have Washington representatives whose main job is to articulate clearly the denomination's position on any of the concerns that come before Congress and federal government agencies. Some even have lobbyists at the state and local levels.

For example, the Religious Action Center of Reform Judaism has maintained a presence in Washington, D.C., for many years, as has the United States Conference of Catholic Bishops, just as many trade groups and industries maintain a lobbying presence in Washington.

Religions also have other means of influencing the government. Individuals, as individuals, can communicate with their elected representatives to express their views; they can also be organized to conduct letter-writing campaigns, to raise (or withhold) political donations, or to vote for or against particular candidates.

> Finally, what of the long-term relationships between religion and politics? Atheists and anticlericals (many regarding themselves as "liberals") like to rehearse the role of the Crusades and Inquisition, wars of religion and U.S. evangelical Christians to exclude the Churches from any involvement in politics. Insofar as there is a debate, this is conducted on the level of alarm aroused when a British prime minister casually mentions that he is accountable to God,…. It is almost superfluous to add that Christianity played an integral part in Europe's high culture, and in such campaigns (or crusades) as abolishing the slave trade or ameliorating social evils of industrialization. How many atheistic liberals run soup kitchens for homeless drug addicts? Is the culture of guns and gangster rap, which thrills progressive cultural commentators, a better alternative to the thriving black Pentecostal churches? More controversially, the Churches upheld necessary inhibitions and taboos, without which we seem degraded, judging by much of what TV commissioning editors regularly inflict upon us in an obsession with sex that they share with some clergy. Christianity's historical achievements deserve more notice than they customarily receive.
>
> Michael Burleigh, *Sacred Causes*, pp. xv–xvi

A number of issues have excited the passions of religious leaders and their constituents over the years. We shall look at some of them now.

CREATIONISM/INTELLIGENT DESIGN

The archenemies of those who promote creationism and intelligent design (they are really the same thing) are those who agree with the widely accepted Darwinian theory of evolution.

The so-called Scopes Monkey Trial in 1925 brought the debate between Darwinism and fundamentalist Christianity to the fore in the American mind. John Thomas Scopes was a schoolteacher who was arrested for violating the Butler Act, a Tennessee statute that forbade the teaching of "any theory that denies the Divine Creation of man as taught in the Bible." The resulting trial was one of the first great media circuses because its legal adversaries were two of the most famous lawyers of the time, William Jennings Bryan, an advocate of creationism, and Clarence Darrow, an agnostic. The trial was subsequently adapted for the stage as *Inherit the Wind* and later became a major motion picture.

For all of the rhetorical fireworks, the trial resolved nothing about creationism. The court's decision revolved around Scopes's technical guilt, which was self-evident. The question of whether the Butler Act had violated the principle of separation between church and state was to have been decided by a higher court, but because Scopes's penalty was commuted, the case was not appealed. The issue has returned as local school boards throughout the country have insisted that the scientifically supported Darwinian theory share equal time in classrooms with the biblical account of Creation.

To promote this strategy, creationists have advanced a notion called intelligent design, which asserts that the world is so wonderful, so complete, so beautifully integrated that it could not have been the result of random events. There had to be some force, God, who deliberately designed it. Intelligent design is merely a different way of discrediting the scientific validity of Darwin and the scientists who followed him.

There is no evidence that those promoting creationism or intelligent design will cease their efforts any time soon. Biblical inerrancy is a central part of their belief system so there is simply too much at stake for them to abandon their efforts.

ABORTION

Regrettably the rights and wrongs of abortion have deteriorated into a battle of bumper sticker slogans. Neither pro-choice nor pro-life, the two advertising-like terms appropriated by the two extremes in the debate, conveys much of the nuanced thinking that should prevail.

Those Christians (and a few Jews, usually Orthodox) who stand against abortion rights and define themselves as pro-life base their argument on the ethical and moral question of when life begins. Does it begin at the moment of conception or at some later stage? Roman Catholics and many other Christians believe that the precise moment that human life begins is when the egg and the sperm join together. Their entire argument follows from this primary premise.

Those who identify themselves as pro-choice base their argument on a woman's right to determine what happens to her own body. This, they say, should be the criterion governing whether a woman chooses to abort her pregnancy or not.

In a sense, the two arguments, each with its own merits, are not even playing on the same field. They pass each other without engagement. And the extremists, whose strident voices dominate the debate, polarize the discussion to such an extent that little conversation is possible.

Jews, by and large, have accepted the notion that the moment of "ensoulment" takes place when the fetus emerges from the woman's womb. Until then, the fetus is an appendage of its mother's body, much like a finger or an arm. Talmudic and later commentators adopted a more conservative stance—that a fetus can only be permissibly aborted for forty days after conception. After forty days, it is deemed to be a separate life and thus entitled to protection. Obviously this opinion is not based on scientific evidence. Orthodox Jews most frequently align themselves with those wishing to limit abortion except in the most extreme cases, usually cases in which the mother's health is in danger.

Those who believe that life begins with conception conclude not only that abortion is wrong, but that any procedure that compromises the viability of the fetus is potentially murder. The 1973 Supreme Court case of *Roe v. Wade* is the flash point for many evangelical and fundamentalist preachers, and for politicians who hold similar views. The finding of the court was that the Texas law making it a crime to assist a woman to get an abortion violated her due process rights under the Fourteenth Amendment to the U.S. Constitution. *Roe v. Wade* concluded that abortions are permissible for any reason a woman chooses, up until the "point at which the fetus becomes 'viable,' that is, potentially able to live outside the mother's womb, albeit with artificial aid. Viability is usually placed at about seven months (28 weeks) but may occur earlier, even at 24 weeks."[2] The court also held that abortion must be available when needed to protect a woman's health, even after the fetus is potentially viable.

Ever since *Roe v. Wade* was decided, there has been constant agitation from pro-life forces for the president to appoint new justices to the Supreme Court who will reverse the decision.

STEM CELLS

Another related and controversial issue is the use of stem cells harvested from human embryos in research to cure diseases such as Parkinson's, Alzheimer's, cerebral palsy, multiple sclerosis, and spinal cord injuries. At the heart of the issue is whether the destruction of the human embryo that results from this process is unethical or immoral—even if the embryo is fated to be destroyed, as in the case of excess embryos resulting from in vitro fertilization techniques.

American public opinion is divided on this issue, which has many complicated scientific ramifications. Several states have set aside funds for this research, despite the serious restrictions on stem cell research imposed by the federal government on projects it funds.

The religious opposition to stem cell research comes essentially from two sources: the Roman Catholic Church and evangelical Christian groups. Their contention is that the moment the egg and the sperm meet, human life begins. Therefore, these potential lives need to be protected. Although the Catholic Church has condemned in vitro fertilization, many evangelical groups have yet to suggest that the process be banned, even though abandoned embryos are an inevitable consequence of the procedure.

EUTHANASIA

The argument against taking the life of a fetus can be extended to the matter of euthanasia, which is assisted dying, either in withholding artificial life support from someone who otherwise can't survive or in assisted suicide.

The case of Terri Schiavo brought the matter to a head. In 1990, Schiavo suffered a heart attack and subsequent severe brain damage as a result of the loss of oxygen. She remained in a vegetative state, subsisting on a feeding tube, with no signs of consciousness and no medical hope that her condition would improve. Her estranged husband, but still legally her husband, requested that the breathing tube be removed. Her parents wanted the life-support apparatus continued.

The argument between Schiavo's parents and husband became public, involving doctors' opinions, several court cases, and ultimately a ruling by the Supreme Court. The case became alarmingly politicized, with two members of the Bush family—Jeb Bush, the governor of Florida, where Schiavo lived, and President George W. Bush—deeply involved.

Kevin Phillips, in his book *American Theocracy*, writes,

> Although [President] Bush took the bold and ultimately unpopular stand in the Terri Schiavo case, bending over backward to insist on continuing her life support, blocking death is not the theological equivalent of enabling birth. The Bible abounds with the killing of those already born, both by God and by lawful authorities. Bush himself, as governor of Texas, sent hundreds of prisoners to the electric chair. Nor has collateral damage to civilians in a "just war" been a problem.[3]

The conservative religious right tried to impose its theology on the nation, including its politicians. With the passage of a congressional resolution that took the Schiavo case out of the jurisdiction of Florida's courts and passed it up to a federal court, it looked like they would win. But the federal court declined to review the case and polls began to show that the American public (by a margin of as much as 75 percent) were angry with the president and Congress for attempting to intervene. This was the first major test of the theological conservatives' power. The politicians quickly withdrew as they found themselves running against public opinion.

MAPLEWOOD, Minn.—Like most pastors who lead thriving evangelical megachurches, the Rev. Gregory A. Boyd was asked frequently to give his blessing—and the church's—to conservative political candidates and causes.

The requests came from church members and visitors alike: Would he please announce a rally against gay marriage during services? Would he introduce a politician from the pulpit? Could members set up a table in the lobby promoting their anti-abortion work? Would the church distribute "voters' guides" that all but endorsed Republican candidates? And with the country at war, please couldn't the church hang an American flag in the sanctuary?

After refusing each time, Mr. Boyd finally became fed up, he said. Before the last presidential election, he preached six sermons called "The Cross and the Sword" in which he said the church should steer clear of politics, give up moralizing on sexual issues, stop claiming the United States as a "Christian nation" and stop glorifying American military campaigns.

"When the church wins the culture wars, it inevitably loses," Mr. Boyd preached. "When it conquers the world, it becomes the world. When you put your trust in the sword, you lose the cross."

Laurie Goodstein, "Disowning Conservative Politics, Evangelical Pastor Rattles Flock," *The New York Times,* July 30, 2006

Sexual Equality and Homosexuality

For centuries, women were considered to be inferior to men. Many conservative Christians prove the point with a quotation from the book of Ephesians 5:21–24: "Be subject to one another out of reverence for Christ. Wives, be subject to your husbands as you are to the Lord. For the husband is the head of the wife just as Christ is the head of the church, the body of which he is the Savior. Just as the church is subject to Christ, so also wives ought to be in everything to their husbands."

In our egalitarian society, for most people this view is no longer acceptable. The role of women in our society has improved but is still in transition. There is still a glass ceiling in the corporate world that prevents even the most qualified women from rising to the same positions of authority as men. While women are much more active in politics than they were fifty years ago, there is still hesitancy among some of the electorate about the election of women to high office.

The same reluctance prevails in the world of religion. The election of the Most Reverend Katharine Jefferts Schori to a nine-year term as the Presiding Bishop of the Episcopal Church in 2006 was a huge step, since the Episcopal Church only began to ordain women priests in 1976. However, there are still Episcopal dioceses that do not accept women as clergy.

And it was only in 1972 that Sally Priesand was ordained as the first woman rabbi in the United States by the Hebrew Union College-Jewish Institute of Religion. Though the Reconstructionist and Conservative movements followed suit, Orthodox Judaism does not accept ordination of women.

The Roman Catholic Church still does not ordain women as priests, although women are taking an ever-larger role in local parishes as the number of male priests continues to fall.

Other denominations are in various stages of fully accepting women as clergy. The picture of sexual equality in the American religious community is still a mixed one. Indeed, human sexuality remains a difficult matter for the religious community, as witnessed by its struggles with the issue of homosexuality.

The current cultural debate in society about issues of gay and lesbian rights is reflected across the spectrum of Christian denominations. Some have declared a policy of inclusion, others exclusion, and many are working to define a position of moderation.

Nevertheless, just as in society, passions run high around this issue. The Anglican Communion remains sharply divided over the issue of the ordination of gay men and women as priests. The 2003 appointment of an openly gay bishop in New Hampshire has raised the level of acrimony to the point of schism. The Evangelical Lutheran Church, the largest Lutheran denomination in the United States, is still undecided about how to deal with gay clergy and their celibacy, or lack thereof.

A similar range of perspectives can be found within Judaism. Since the early 1970s, the Reform Jewish movement has admitted openly gay men and women and transsexuals to its rabbinical seminaries and cantorial training programs. These men and women serve in congregations all over the United States and Canada. The Reconstructionist movement has done the same. The Conservative movement, through its principal seminary, The Jewish Theological Seminary, is moving toward acceptance of openly gay men and women, and the rabbinical school of the American Jewish University (formerly the University of Judaism) already accepts them in its program. Although there are a few openly gay Orthodox rabbis—they are people who "came out" after ordination—the Orthodox community is unwelcoming to gays and lesbians.

CHANGE IN THE WIND

Needless to say, the vast majority of fundamentalist churches, as well as Orthodox Judaism, remain unalterably opposed to homosexuality. They regard it as a sin and a personal life choice. But they may well find themselves in as awkward and isolated a position as their ancestors did when they resisted the move to abolish slavery in the United States in the years before the Civil War. Change in religious attitudes is slow, even glacial. But it is clear that the general acceptance of women in leadership roles and gay and lesbian men and women as full members of society will have a tremendous impact on religious attitudes and values. Selectively quoting Bible verses to validate previously held positions does not seem adequate any longer, any more than the citation of a few Bible verses to justify slavery.

11

WHAT MIGHT THE
FUTURE HOLD?

NO ONE CAN PREDICT THE FUTURE. But here are some calcu-
lated guesses as to new directions for the American Christian
community. Note that I specify "American." The future of religion in Europe is much harder to predict. The antireligious
feeling in most of Europe seems fairly well entrenched. It
remains to be seen what effect, if any, Pope Benedict XVI's
efforts to "re-Christianize" Europe will have.

But in the United States, certain things seem fairly sure.

- While there may still be some pronouncements
  from the Southern Baptists and a few other
  Protestant groups about converting the Jews, most
  of these efforts seem destined to be extremely limited in their effect.
- Evangelical churches will remain a major part of
  the American scene, but the death of Jerry Falwell,
  and of other prominent fundamentalist preachers,
  and the disgrace of others, may serve to halt the
  stridency. Softer voices are beginning to be heard,
  voices that are more sensitive to human needs than
  to ideology.
- The renewed interest of some evangelicals, such as
  Rick Warren, in community efforts, together with
  the development of the emergent churches, will

grow into a larger movement that will respond to a wide variety of communal needs. The current narrow agenda will be broadened. There are many problems in America that are not "liberal" or "conservative" but that need to be solved. As the megachurches evolve, new alliances are possible with mainstream Protestant churches, Catholics, Jews, and Muslims.

- The various crises in the Roman Catholic Church (sexual abuse and shortages of clergy, among others) may allow some of the more liberal voices in the American Church to be heard with more effect. Catholics and Jews will continue to work together in substantial ways, talking about difficult subjects that we previously avoided.

- Jews don't have much to worry about in relation to Christian anti-Semitism, at least on an institutional or systemic level. The Jewish defense agencies will continue to raise alarms about anti-Semitism, and surveys will continue to show anti-Semitic attitudes among a surprising number of Americans. Except for these individual, hardcore lunatics, however, anti-Semitism as a social force is largely dead in the United States.

- Religion will remain a strong force on the American scene.

Robert Wright, in an April 2007 op-ed piece in *The New York Times*, wrote:

Consider a teaching of Jesus that seems on its surface devoid of strategic import. "You have heard that it was said, 'You shall love your neighbor and hate your enemy.'

But I say to you, love your enemies and pray for those who persecute you."

Christians often cast this verse as innovation, a sharp break from Jesus's Jewish tradition. But the same idea can be found in the Hebrew Bible (the Old Testament), and here it is clear that the point of kindness is to thwart the enemy: "If your enemies are hungry, give them bread to eat; and if they are thirsty, give them water to drink."[1]

Every religion in the United States has been shaped and reshaped by the American experience, including immigration, the vastness of the continent, responses to Europe, both positive and negative, and the growth patterns of the country. The religious experience here is different from any place in the world. It is often said that Europeans really don't understand us. That is a truism that demonstrates its validity daily.

Rome doesn't really "get" the American church. Israelis really don't fully grasp what motivates the American Jewish community. African Anglicans don't understand "those Americans" in the Episcopal Church.

Dynamism means unpredictability. We have begun a new era in American religious life and in Christian-Jewish relations, an era far better than all that came before.

Is the best of times yet to come?

APPENDIX 1

DABRU EMET

A Jewish Statement on
Christians and Christianity

In recent years, there has been a dramatic and unprecedented shift in Jewish and Christian relations. Throughout the nearly two millennia of Jewish exile, Christians have tended to characterize Judaism as a failed religion or, at best, a religion that prepared the way for, and is completed in, Christianity. In the decades since the Holocaust, however, Christianity has changed dramatically. An increasing number of official Church bodies, both Roman Catholic and Protestant, have made public statements of their remorse about Christian mistreatment of Jews and Judaism. These statements have declared, furthermore, that Christian teaching and preaching can and must be reformed so that they acknowledge God's enduring covenant with the Jewish people and celebrate the contribution of Judaism to world civilization and to Christian faith itself.

We believe these changes merit a thoughtful Jewish response. Speaking only for ourselves—an interdenominational group of Jewish scholars—we believe it is time for Jews to learn about the efforts of Christians to honor Judaism. We believe it is time for Jews to reflect on what Judaism may now say about Christianity. As a first step, we offer eight brief statements about how Jews and Christians may relate to one another.

Jews and Christians worship the same God. Before the rise of Christianity, Jews were the only worshippers of the God of Israel. But Christians also worship the God of Abraham, Isaac, and Jacob; creator of heaven and earth. While Christian worship is not a viable religious choice for Jews, as Jewish theologians we rejoice that, through Christianity, hundreds of millions of people have entered into relationship with the God of Israel.

Jews and Christians seek authority from the same book—the Bible (what Jews call "Tanakh" and Christians call the "Old Testament"). Turning to it for religious orientation, spiritual enrichment, and communal education, we each take away similar lessons: God created and sustains the universe; God established a covenant with the people Israel, God's revealed word guides Israel to a life of righteousness; and God will ultimately redeem Israel and the whole world. Yet, Jews and Christians interpret the Bible differently on many points. Such differences must always be respected.

Christians can respect the claim of the Jewish people upon the Land of Israel. The most important event for Jews since the Holocaust has been the reestablishment of a Jewish state in the Promised Land. As members of a biblically based religion, Christians appreciate that Israel was promised—and given—to Jews as the physical center of the covenant between them and God. Many Christians support the State of Israel for reasons far more profound than mere politics. As Jews, we applaud this support. We also recognize that Jewish tradition mandates justice for all non-Jews who reside in a Jewish state.

Jews and Christians accept the moral principles of Torah. Central to the moral principles of Torah is the inalienable sanctity and dignity of every human being. All of us were created in the image of God. This shared moral emphasis can be the basis of an improved relationship between our two communities. It can also be the basis of a powerful witness to all humanity for improving the lives of our fellow human beings and for standing against the immoralities and idolatries that harm and degrade us. Such witness is especially needed after the unprecedented horrors of the past century.

Nazism was not a Christian phenomenon. Without the long history of Christian anti-Judaism and Christian violence against Jews, Nazi ideology could not have taken hold nor could it have been carried out. Too many Christians participated in, or were sympathetic to, Nazi atrocities against Jews. Other Christians did not protest sufficiently against these atrocities. But Nazism itself was not an inevitable outcome of Christianity. If the Nazi extermination of the Jews had been fully successful, it would have turned its murderous rage more directly to Christians. We recognize with gratitude those Christians who risked or sacrificed their lives to save Jews during the Nazi regime. With that in mind, we encourage the continuation of recent efforts in Christian theology to repudiate unequivocally contempt of Judaism and the Jewish people. We applaud those Christians who reject this teaching of contempt, and we do not blame them for the sins committed by their ancestors.

The humanly irreconcilable difference between Jews and Christians will not be settled until God redeems the entire world as promised in Scripture. Christians know and serve God through Jesus Christ and the Christian tradition. Jews know and serve God through Torah and the

Jewish tradition. That difference will not be settled by one community insisting that it has interpreted Scripture more accurately than the other; nor by exercising political power over the other. Jews can respect Christians' faithfulness to their revelation just as we expect Christians to respect our faithfulness to our revelation. Neither Jew nor Christian should be pressed into affirming the teaching of the other community.

A new relationship between Jews and Christians will not weaken Jewish practice. An improved relationship will not accelerate the cultural and religious assimilation that Jews rightly fear. It will not change traditional Jewish forms of worship, nor increase intermarriage between Jews and non-Jews, nor persuade more Jews to convert to Christianity, nor create a false blending of Judaism and Christianity. We respect Christianity as a faith that originated within Judaism and that still has significant contacts with it. We do not see it as an extension of Judaism. Only if we cherish our own traditions can we pursue this relationship with integrity.

Jews and Christians must work together for justice and peace. Jews and Christians, each in their own way, recognize the unredeemed state of the world as reflected in the persistence of persecution, poverty, and human degradation and misery. Although justice and peace are finally God's, our joint efforts, together with those of other faith communities, will help bring the kingdom of God for which we hope and long. Separately and together, we must work to bring justice and peace to our world. In this enterprise, we are guided by the vision of the prophets of Israel:

> It shall come to pass in the end of days that the mountain
> of the Lord's house shall be established at the top of the

mountains and be exalted above the hills, and the nations shall flow unto it ... and many peoples shall go and say, "Come ye and let us go up to the mountain of the Lord to the house of the God of Jacob and He will teach us of His ways and we will walk in his paths." (Isaiah 2:2–3)

Tikva Frymer-Kensky, University of Chicago
David Novak, University of Toronto
Peter Ochs, University of Virginia
Michael Signer, University of Notre Dame

Note: Dabru Emet was published in the *New York Times* on September 10, 2000, and was endorsed by more than 150 prominent Jewish scholars and rabbis of all denominations.

NOSTRA AETATE

**Declaration on the Relation of the Church
to Non-Christian Religions**
Nostra Aetate
**Proclaimed by his Holiness
Pope Paul VI
On October 28, 1965**

1. In our time, when day by day mankind is being drawn closer together, and the ties between different peoples are becoming stronger, the Church examines more closely the relationship to non-Christian religions. In her task of promoting unity and love among men, indeed among nations, she considers above all in this declaration what men have in common and what draws them to fellowship.

One is the community of all peoples, one their origin, for God made the whole human race to live over the face of the earth.[1] One also is their final goal, God. His providence, His manifestations of goodness, His saving design extend to all men,[2] until that time when the elect will be united in the Holy City, the city ablaze with the glory of God, where the nations will walk in His light.[3]

Men expect from the various religions answers to the unsolved riddles of the human condition, which today, even as in former times, deeply stir the hearts of men: What is man? What is the meaning, the aim of our life? What is moral good, what sin? Whence suffering and what purpose does it serve? Which is the road to true happiness? What are death, judgment and retribution after death? What, finally, is that ultimate inexpressible mystery which encompasses our existence: whence do we come, and where are we going?

2. From ancient times down to the present, there is found among various peoples a certain perception of that hidden power which hovers over the course of things and over the events of human history; at times some indeed have come to the recognition of a Supreme Being, or even of a Father. This perception and recognition penetrates their lives with a profound religious sense.

Religions, however, that are bound up with an advanced culture have struggled to answer the same questions by means of more refined concepts and a more developed language. Thus in Hinduism, men contemplate the divine mystery and express it through an inexhaustible abundance of myths and through searching philosophical inquiry. They seek freedom from the anguish of our human condition either through ascetical practices or profound meditation or a flight to God with love and trust. Again, Buddhism, in its various forms, realizes the radical insufficiency of this changeable world; it teaches a way by which men, in a devout and confident spirit, may be able either to acquire the state of perfect liberation, or attain, by their own efforts or through higher help, supreme illumination. Likewise, other religions found everywhere try to counter the restlessness of the human heart, each in its own manner, by proposing "ways," comprising teachings, rules of life, and sacred rites. The Catholic Church rejects nothing that is true and holy in these religions. She regards with sincere reverence those ways of conduct and of life, those precepts and teachings which, though differing in many aspects from the ones she holds and sets forth, nonetheless often reflect a ray of that Truth which enlightens all men. Indeed, she proclaims, and ever must proclaim Christ "the way, the truth, and the life" (John 14:6), in whom men may find the fullness of religious life, in whom God has reconciled all things to Himself.[4]

The Church, therefore, exhorts her sons, that through dialogue and collaboration with the followers of other religions, carried out with prudence and love and in witness to the Christian faith and life, they recognize, preserve and promote the good things, spiritual and moral, as well as the socio-cultural values found among these men.

3. The Church regards with esteem also the Moslems. They adore the one God, living and subsisting in Himself; merciful and all-powerful, the Creator of heaven and earth,[5] who has spoken to men; they take pains to submit wholeheartedly to even His inscrutable decrees, just as Abraham, with whom the faith of Islam takes pleasure in linking itself, submitted to God. Though they do not acknowledge Jesus as God, they revere Him as a prophet. They also honor Mary, His virgin Mother; at times they even call on her with devotion. In addition, they await the day of judgment when God will render their deserts to all those who have been raised up from the dead. Finally, they value the moral life and worship God especially through prayer, almsgiving and fasting.

Since in the course of centuries not a few quarrels and hostilities have arisen between Christians and Moslems, this sacred synod urges all to forget the past and to work sincerely for mutual understanding and to preserve as well as to promote together for the benefit of all mankind social justice and moral welfare, as well as peace and freedom.

4. As the sacred synod searches into the mystery of the Church, it remembers the bond that spiritually ties the people of the New Covenant to Abraham's stock.

Thus the Church of Christ acknowledges that, according to God's saving design, the beginnings of her faith and her election are found already among the Patriarchs, Moses

and the prophets. She professes that all who believe in
Christ—Abraham's sons according to faith[6]—are included in
the same Patriarch's call, and likewise that the salvation of the
Church is mysteriously foreshadowed by the chosen people's
exodus from the land of bondage. The Church, therefore,
cannot forget that she received the revelation of the Old
Testament through the people with whom God in His inexpressible mercy concluded the Ancient Covenant. Nor can
she forget that she draws sustenance from the root of that
well-cultivated olive tree onto which have been grafted the
wild shoots, the Gentiles.[7] Indeed, the Church believes that
by His cross Christ, Our Peace, reconciled Jews and Gentiles,
making both one in Himself.[8]

The Church keeps ever in mind the words of the Apostle
about his kinsmen:"theirs is the sonship and the glory and the
covenants and the law and the worship and the promises;
theirs are the fathers and from them is the Christ according to
the flesh" (Rom. 9:4-5), the Son of the Virgin Mary. She also
recalls that the Apostles, the Church's main-stay and pillars, as
well as most of the early disciples who proclaimed Christ's
Gospel to the world, sprang from the Jewish people.

As Holy Scripture testifies, Jerusalem did not recognize
the time of her visitation,[9] nor did the Jews in large number,
accept the Gospel; indeed not a few opposed its spreading.[10]
Nevertheless, God holds the Jews most dear for the sake of
their Fathers; He does not repent of the gifts He makes or of
the calls He issues—such is the witness of the Apostle.[11] In
company with the Prophets and the same Apostle, the
Church awaits that day, known to God alone, on which all
peoples will address the Lord in a single voice and "serve him
shoulder to shoulder" (Soph. 3:9).[12]

Since the spiritual patrimony common to Christians
and Jews is thus so great, this sacred synod wants to foster and

recommend that mutual understanding and respect which is the fruit, above all, of biblical and theological studies as well as of fraternal dialogues.

True, the Jewish authorities and those who followed their lead pressed for the death of Christ;[13] still, what happened in His passion cannot be charged against all the Jews, without distinction, then alive, nor against the Jews of today. Although the Church is the new people of God, the Jews should not be presented as rejected or accursed by God, as if this followed from the Holy Scriptures. All should see to it, then, that in catechetical work or in the preaching of the word of God they do not teach anything that does not conform to the truth of the Gospel and the spirit of Christ.

Furthermore, in her rejection of every persecution against any man, the Church, mindful of the patrimony she shares with the Jews and moved not by political reasons but by the Gospel's spiritual love, decries hatred, persecutions, displays of anti-Semitism, directed against Jews at any time and by anyone.

Besides, as the Church has always held and holds now, Christ underwent His passion and death freely, because of the sins of men and out of infinite love, in order that all may reach salvation. It is, therefore, the burden of the Church's preaching to proclaim the cross of Christ as the sign of God's all-embracing love and as the fountain from which every grace flows.

5. We cannot truly call on God, the Father of all, if we refuse to treat in a brotherly way any man, created as he is in the image of God. Man's relation to God the Father and his relation to men his brothers are so linked together that Scripture says: "He who does not love does not know God" (1 John 4:8).

No foundation therefore remains for any theory or practice that leads to discrimination between man and man or people and people, so far as their human dignity and the rights flowing from it are concerned.

The Church reproves, as foreign to the mind of Christ, any discrimination against men or harassment of them because of their race, color, condition of life, or religion. On the contrary, following in the footsteps of the holy Apostles Peter and Paul, this sacred synod ardently implores the Christian faithful to "maintain good fellowship among the nations" (1 Peter 2:12), and, if possible, to live for their part in peace with all men,[14] so that they may truly be sons of the Father who is in heaven.[15]

Notes

1. Cf. *Acts* 17:26
2. Cf. *Wis.* 8:1; *Acts* 14:17; *Rom.* 2:6-7; 1 *Tim.* 2:4
3. Cf. *Apoc.* 21:23f.
4. Cf. 2 *Cor.* 5:18-19
5. Cf. St. Gregory VII, *letter XXI to Anzir (Nacir), King of Mauritania* (Pl. 148, col. 450f.)
6. Cf. *Gal.* 3:7
7. Cf. *Rom.* 11:17-24
8. Cf. *Eph.* 2:14-16
9. Cf. *Lk.* 19:44
10. Cf. *Rom.* 11:28
11. Cf. *Rom.* 11:28-29; cf. dogmatic Constitution, *Lumen Gentium* (Light of nations) AAS, 57 (1965) pag. 20
12. Cf. *Is.* 66:23; *Ps.* 65:4; *Rom.* 11:11-32
13. Cf. *John.* 19:6
14. Cf. *Rom.* 12:1
15. Cf. *Matt.* 5:45

NOTES

CHAPTER 2

1. McFadyen, *Bound to Sin*, 16.
2. Deuteronomy 30:19–20.
3. *Gates of Repentance*, 516.
4. Borowitz, *Renewing the Covenant*.
5. Ibid.

CHAPTER 3

1. Meeks, Wayne A., in "From Jesus to Christ: The First Christians—Wrestling with Their Jewish Heritage," http://www.pbs.org/wgbh/pages/frontline/shows/religion/first/wrestling.html.
2. Talbert, *Reading Acts*.
3. *Catechism of the Catholic Church* (1994), 118.
4. Armstrong, *A History of God*, 114.
5. "The Blessed Trinity," http://www.newadvent.org/cathen/15047a.htm.

CHAPTER 4

1. Jones, *On Musicals, Ourselves*, 152, 203.
2. Brettler, *How to Read the Bible*, 150.
3. Rabbi Michael Cook quoted in *Los Angeles Times,* April 3, 2007.

CHAPTER 5

1. Friedman, *Who Wrote the Bible?*, 53.
2. Feldman, "Orthodox Paradox," *New York Times Magazine*, July 22, 2007.
3. Stringfellow, *A Brief Examination of Scripture Testimony on the Institution of Slavery*, 136–167.
4. Ibid.
5. Weld, *The Bible Against Slavery*.
6. Douglass, *Narrative in the Life of Frederick Douglass*.
7. "The Baptist Faith and Message," http://www.sbc.net/bfm/bfm2000.asp.

CHAPTER 6

1. Green, "Messiah in Judaism," *Judaisms and their Messiahs*, 1–14.

CHAPTER 7

1. Kohler, *Jewish Theology*, 5.
2. *Nostra Aetate,* section 4.
3. *Catechism of the Catholic Church* (1994), 223.
4. "Declaration of the Evangelical Lutheran Church in America to the Jewish Community," http://www.elca.org/ecumenical/interreligious/jewish/declaration.html.
5. United Methodist Church position paper, "Building New Bridges in Hope," http://archives.umc.org/interior.asp?ptid=4&mid=3301.
6. Ibid.
7. "How Christians View Non-Christian Religions: Statements by Christians," http://www.religioustolerance.org/chr_othe2.htm.
8. "Conservative Christians: Statements about Jewish Conversion," http://www.religioustolerance.org/chr_jcon2.htm.
9. "How Christians View Non-Christian Religions: Statements by Christians," http://www.religioustolerance.org/chr_othe2.htm.

CHAPTER 8

1. Laqueur, *A History of Zionism*, 6.
2. Ibid, 7.

3. Ibid, 18.
4. Herzl, *The Jewish State.*
5. "Proclamation of the 3rd International Christian Zionist Congress," http://christianactionforisrael.org/congress.html.
6. "Union for Reform Judaism Board of Trustees Meeting, Remarks by Rabbi Eric H. Yoffie, June 10, 2007; Seattle, Washington," http://urj.org/Articles/index.cfm?id=15098.
7. Mead, "God's Country?" *Foreign Affairs*, 41.

CHAPTER 9

1. http://hirr.hartsem.edu/research/fastfacts/fast_facts.html#largest.
2. FritzGerald, "The Evangelical Surprise," *New York Review of Books*.

CHAPTER 10

1. Lilla, "The Politics of God," http://www.nytimes.com/2007/08/19/magazine/19Religion-t.html?_r=1&pagewanted=4&em&ei=5087&en=a098a9ed1ed27038&ex=1187668800&adxnnlx=1187539536-F/IPEnsmMki4bnoBgzAVDQ&oref=slogin.
2. *Roe v. Wade*, 410 U.S. 113 (1973).
3. Phillips, *American Theocracy*, 242.

CHAPTER 11

1. Wright, "An Easter Sermon," *The New York Times*, http://select.nytimes.com/2007/04/07/opinion/07wright.html?scp=1&sq=robert+wright+an+easter+sermon&st=nyt.

A Glossary of Christian Terms

As previously noted, this is not intended to be a complete glossary of Christian theological and worship terms. It is intended only as a basic primer to facilitate the reader's understanding of the material discussed in this book.

Worship Services

Altar—The table at the front of the church, in the Chancel area, where the Communion ritual is performed, and in Roman Catholic churches, where most of the service takes place. A re-creation of the altar described in the biblical books of Leviticus and Numbers as the site of animal sacrifices. In many Protestant churches where communion is not viewed as a re-enactment of a sacrifice, it is called the "table" or "communion table."

Baptism—A Christian version of an ancient Jewish water purification ritual. Usually performed on infants as an initiation rite into Christianity. However, Baptists believe that the candidates should have already attained the age of reason. Some believe that it is a salvation rite, redeeming one from hell. It is the first of the Christian sacraments.

Cardinal—One of the over one hundred counselors to the pope in Rome, almost always a bishop. The College of Cardinals convenes to elect a new pope upon the death of the current pope, but cardinals over the age of eighty do not have a vote. Bishops who are the heads of large Roman Catholic archdioceses in the United States, such as those in New York, Los Angeles, Boston, Philadelphia, and Chicago, are usually named cardinals, but not all cardinals are bishops—a cardinal may be simply a priest.

Celebrant—The clergy conducting a worship service where Communion is performed.

Chancel—The area at the front of a church, where the altar or communion table is located.

Clerical Titles—Reverend (Rev.) is the correct title for most Christian clergy. In Episcopal churches, the head of the local church is usually called "rector," from the Latin *rex*, for king. Vicar is usually the second in command, or the head of a small parish. In cathedrals, the head (or rector) is called "dean." Other members of the clergy in cathedrals are called "canons," as in the Rev. John Doe, canon pastor. Deans of cathedrals are called "very reverend." Bishops, the "right reverend." Curates are assistant clergy, usually recently out of seminary in their first jobs.

Communion/Eucharist—The high point in many Christian worship services, this is a re-enactment of the Last Supper, thought to be the Passover seder, that includes the eating of bread (called by Jesus "my body"; see "wafer," below) and drinking of wine or grape juice (called by Jesus "my blood"; see "wine/grape juice," below). *Eucharist* is Greek for "thanksgiving" and refers to communion with God. Baptism is often required for participation. Interpretations vary concerning what precisely takes place during communion with regard to the elements of bread and wine. (For two common interpretations, see "consubstantiation" and "transubstantiation" below.)

Consubstantiation (also see "transubstantiation," below)—The basic view of communion held by the majority of Protestant denominations. The bread and wine are believed to exist *with* (Latin-"con") the actual body and blood of Jesus. In other words, it's not a complete transformation (see "transubstantiation") from one to the other, but both are truly present (bread and body; wine and blood).

Cross/Crucifix—The cross is the most potent symbol of Christian belief. The crucifix has an image of Jesus nailed to the cross and usually signifies a Roman Catholic church. An "empty" cross (representing the resurrected Jesus) usually signifies a Protestant church. A crucifer is the person carrying the cross in church processions.

Diocese—An administrative area of the Roman Catholic or Episcopal Church. It might be a state, or for larger population centers, a city and its environs. The head of the diocese is the bishop. Many larger dioceses and those of historical importance are known as Archdioceses. The head of the archdiocese is an archbishop.

Gospels—The first four books of the New Testament—Matthew, Mark, Luke, and John—depicting Jesus's life and works.

Mass—or Eucharist, the two-part ritual, led by a priest, of publicly reading the Bible and then offering bread and wine in imitation of Jesus at the Last Supper. The word "Mass" probably comes from the Latin root of the word "dismissal" used at the end of the service.

Missal—The book of prayers used by the priest at the altar during Mass.

New Testament—the twenty-seven books that make up the second "half" of the Christian Bible. It contains the four Gospels (Matthew, Mark, Luke, and John) numerous letters ("missives") from the apostle Paul and others to first-century Christians and their churches, and other literature, such as the apocalyptic book of Revelation. The first "half" is the Hebrew Bible, usually referred to as the "Old Testament."

Sacraments—The essential symbolic rituals of the Christian Church. Roman Catholics celebrate and affirm seven sacraments: baptism, confirmation, penance, communion, marriage, last rites and ordination. Protestants generally celebrate and affirm two sacraments: baptism and communion.

Thurible/Thurifer—The thurible is a vessel used to broadcast incense around the altar during worship services. The "thurifer" is the person using the thurible.

Transubstantiation (see also "consubstantiation," above)—The term used for the *literal and mystical* transformation of the bread and the wine used in communion into the actual body and blood of Christ. This is the view held by the Roman Catholic Chuch.

Verger—The chief usher in Episcopal churches who leads the processions and makes certain that the services are conducted properly.

Vestments—The ritual clothing worn by priests and other officials in the performance of the rituals of Christian worship. In some denominations, a sash worn diagonally across the chest signifies a deacon, a lower order of clergy who is not a priest. The colors of the vestments change according to the seasons of the liturgical year, as do the altar decorations.

Wafer—The bread used in some Christian services for Communion. The Christian re-creation of the matzah used at the seder. Called by Jesus "my body." See Matthew 26:26f.; Mark 14:22f.; Luke 22:19f. Many Protestant denominations use yeasted bread.

Wine/Grape Juice—The drink used at a Protestant Communion service or a Catholic Mass in imitation of Jesus at the Last Supper. Catholic practice allows only for wine or mustum.

THEOLOGICAL TERMS

Born Again—A term sometimes used by Christians to indicate a concious decision to become a Christian, often described as "accepting Jesus as my personal Lord and Savior." Often associated particularly with evangelical Christianity, the phrase occurs in John 3:3.

Dispensationalism—Dispensationalists believe that human history is divided into seven different time periods (or dispensations).

During each dispensation, God deals with humanity in a manner unique to that dispensation. These eras are the Garden of Eden, Adam to Noah, Noah to Abraham, Abraham to Moses, Moses to Jesus, Jesus to Judgment Day, and the millennial kingdom.

Evangelical—A loose term describing Protestant Christians sharing certain traits, such as an emphasis on evangelizing and a high regard for the Bible.

Fundamentalism—As a distinct movement, fundamentalism developed in the United States at the beginning of the 20th century as a response to the growing rationalism that had become popular among Christians. It asserted these fundamental tenets of belief: the inerrancy of the Bible, the divinity of Jesus, the virgin birth, vicarious atonement of Jesus, physical resurrection and the return of Jesus at a future time to judge humanity.

Luther, Martin—German, 1483–1546. One of the principle leaders of the Reformation in Germany, Luther's protests against the abuses of the Roman Catholic Church led to his excommunication as a priest, and further to the rise of Protestantism. He believed that salvation would come through faith in Jesus, unmediated by the Roman Catholic Church. He also translated the Bible into German, an important step in moving away from the authority of the Vatican, allowing many more people to read and understand the Bible by themselves.

Mainline Churches—A term generally used to describe the non-evangelical, non-fundamentalist churches that were traditionally the mainstay of Protestant Christianity in the United States. The churches generally included are the Episcopal Church, the Presbyterian Church, the United Methodist Church, United Church of Christ (Congregationalists), Evangelical Lutheran Church, and the Christian Church.

Reformation—The movement led by Martin Luther in the early sixteenth century that led to the development of Protestant churches in Europe. Other leaders in the Reformation were John Knox

(1514–1572), Ulrich Zwingli (1484–1531), John Calvin (1509–1564), and Thomas Cranmer (1489–1556).

Revelation, Book of—The final book of the New Testament, filled with many apocalyptic and mysterious images. Similar to some Jewish apocalyptic works such as the book of Daniel, it became the focus of the interest of fundamentalists and evangelicals who predict Jesus's return to earth, where they believe he will rule for one thousand years.

Second Coming—This term generally refers to the belief that Jesus, dissatisfied with the sinful condition of human beings, will come again, a time accompanied by immense worldwide suffering, called the tribulation. According to some fundamentalist and evangelical thinkers and writers, those who are "born again" will be literally lifted up from the earth and taken from the world when the tribulation marking the Second Coming occurs. This lifting up is called "rapture," and those lifted up will not suffer any of the ill effects caused by this period of tribulation.

SUGGESTIONS FOR
FURTHER READING

THIS IS A HIGHLY SELECTIVE list for those who wish to delve more deeply into the worlds of Christianity and Judaism.

Abba Hillel Silver, *Where Judaism Differed: An Inquiry into the Distinctiveness of Judaism*. Philadelphia: Jewish Publication Society, 1957.

> Alas, this book is out of print, but if you can find it, read it. Rabbi Silver compares Judaism with the main religions of the world. He writes beautifully, clearly, and does not speak down to the reader.

Huston Smith, *The Soul of Christianity: Restoring the Great Tradition*. San Francisco: HarperCollins, 2005.

> Huston Smith is the dean of religion scholars in America. Born in 1919 in China, the son of missionaries, he taught at the University of California at Berkeley, Syracuse University, the Massachusetts Institute of Technology, and Washington University. This is a very gentle book. It is short, but complete in many ways. It is a contrast to the hard-edged sermons and books by evangelicals who have all the answers to human woes.

Marc Zvi Brettler, *How to Read the Bible*. Philadelphia: Jewish Publication Society, 2005.

> Brettler, a professor at Brandeis University, has written a thoughtful and helpful book for those who want to understand the Jewish approach to biblical scholarship. Among the topics he deals with at length are the Creation stories, the Bible as myth, and the role of the prophets. This book will give the reader a complete set of armor to help deal with the biblical literalists.

Amy-Jill Levine, *The Misunderstood Jew: The Church and the Scandal of the Jewish Jesus*. San Francisco: HarperCollins, 2006.

> Levine, professor of New Testament at Vanderbilt University Divinity School in Nashville, Tennessee, is a brilliant teacher and lecturer. One of her special themes has been to understand how Jesus has been pulled out of his Jewish context, which has resulted in an intolerant understanding of Jews, and sometimes hatred. She shows how Christian scholars often strove to make Judaism seem antiquated so that Christianity could look superior.

Rabbi Samuel Sandmel, *A Jewish Understanding of the New Testament*. Woodstock, VT: SkyLight Paths Publishing, 2005.

> Without compromising his Jewish identity or encouraging any traditional Jewish stereotypes about the New Testament, Rabbi Sandmel offers an enlightened view of Christian beliefs and encourages readers to acknowledge their common humanity with people of all religions.

Rabbi Samuel Sandmel, *We Jews and Jesus: Exploring Theological Differences for Mutual Understanding*. Woodstock, VT: SkyLight Paths Publishing, 2006.

> This candid look at the what and why of the Jewish attitude toward Jesus is a clear exposition for both Christians and Jews.

Rabbi Michael J. Cook, *Modern Jews Engage the New Testament: Enhancing Jewish Well-Being in a Christian Environment.* Woodstock, VT: Jewish Lights Publishing, 2008.

> This in-depth volume offers an unprecedented solution-oriented introduction to Jesus and Paul, the Gospels and Revelation, leading Jews out of anxieties that plague them. Accessible to lay people, scholars, and clergy of all faiths, it includes innovative teaching aids that make it ideal for rabbis and other educators.

Kevin Phillips, *American Theocracy: The Peril and Politics of Radical Religion, Oil, and Borrowed Money in the 21ˢᵗ Century.* New York: Viking Penguin, 2006.

> In this highly tendentious book, Phillips lays bare the political alliance between the Republican party and the evangelical Christian right. The author, a former Republican strategist, shows how the surge of fundamentalism coincides with the rise in apocalyptic thinking by American politicians.

Julie Galambush. *The Reluctant Parting: How the New Testament's Jewish Writers Created a Christian Book.* San Francisco: HarperCollins, 2005.

> Peeling away centuries of misinterpretation, *The Reluctant Parting* tells the painful story of how the New Testament authors fought—ultimately in vain—to preserve their legitimacy as members of the Jewish community. Biblical scholar Julie Galambush, a former Baptist minister who converted to Judaism, reveals the diversity within first-century Judaism and how an intra-Jewish debate about what it means to be Jewish included the followers of Jesus as one Jewish sect among many.

Walter Laqueur, *A History of Zionism: From the French Revolution to the Establishment of the State of Israel*. New York: Holt, Rinehart and Winston, 1972.

> Historian Laqueur has written a brilliant and insightful history, taking the reader from Zionism's origins in the Enlightenment and the French Revolution to the establishment of the State of Israel. If you want to understand what Zionism is about, this is a must for your reading list.

Stuart M. Matlins and Arthur J. Magida, *How to Be a Perfect Stranger: The Essential Religious Etiquette Handbook*, 4th ed. Woodstock, VT: SkyLight Paths Publishing, 2006.

> Covering all of the major and many of the minor religions in America, this volume is extremely helpful if you are planning to visit a church or synagogue that is unfamiliar to you. The authors have done a masterful and comprehensive job of giving you all the information you need to avoid embarrassment to yourself or your hosts, including a brief summary of the religion's history and theology. Included are appropriate procedures for attendance at weddings or funerals and other ceremonies and observances.

F. E. Peters, *The Voice, the Word, the Books: The Sacred Scripture of the Jews, Christians, and Muslims*. Princeton, NJ: Princeton University Press, 2007.

> Frank Peters's newest book is a masterpiece. His summary of the Hebrew Bible, the New Testament, and the Qur'an is outstanding. He writes beautifully, tracing the history of the individual texts, the evolution of the biblical canon, and the changing ways they have been read.

Robert G. Clouse, *The End of Days: Essential Selections from Apocalyptic Texts—Annotated & Explained*. Woodstock, VT: SkyLight Paths Publishing, 2007.

This highly accessible and informative book helps you understand the complex Christian visions of the end of the world, from the earliest writings of the church fathers through popular books circulating in our own day, including the mega-bestselling *Left Behind* series of novels.

BIBLIOGRAPHY

Armstrong, Karen. *A History of God: The 4,000-Year Quest of Judaism, Christianity and Islam.* New York: Knopf, 1993.

Baeck, Leo. *The Essence of Judaism.* New York: Schocken, 1967.

Borowitz, Eugene B. *Renewing the Covenant: A Theology for the Postmodern Jew.* Philadelphia: Jewish Publication Society, 1991.

Brettler, Marc Zvi. *How to Read the Bible.* Philadelphia: Jewish Publication Society, 2005.

Burgon, Dean John William. *Essays and Reviews,* 1860.

Burleigh, Michael. *Sacred Causes: The Clash of Religion and Politics, from the Great War to the War on Terror.* Great Britain: Harper Press, 2006.

Calvin, John. *Christianae Religionis Institutio* [Institutes of the Christian Religion]. 1559.

Campbell, Joseph. *The Hero with a Thousand Faces.* Princeton, NJ: Princeton University Press, 1949.

Campbell, Joseph. *Occidental Mythology.* New York: Viking Penguin, 1964.

Dershowitz, Alan. *The Genesis of Justice: Ten Stories of Biblical Injustice that Led to the Ten Commandments and Modern Morality and Law.* New York: Warner Books, 2000.

Douglass, Frederick. *Narrative of the Life of Frederick Douglass, an American Slave.* 1845.

Elukin, Jonathan. *Living Together, Living Apart: Rethinking Jewish-Christian Relations in the Middle Ages.* Princeton, NJ: Princeton University Press, 2007.

Feldman, Noah. "Orthodox Paradox." *New York Times Magazine,* July 22, 2007.

Friedman, Richard Elliot. *Who Wrote the Bible?* New York: Summit Books, 1987.

FritzGerald, Frances, "The Evangelical Surprise." *New York Review of Books,* April 26, 2007.

Frymer-Kensky, Tikva, David Novak, Peter Ochs, David Fox Sandmel, and Michael A. Signer, eds. *Christianity in Jewish Terms.* Boulder, CO: Westview Press, 2000.

Goodstein, Laurie. "Disowning Conservative Politics, Evangelical Pastor Rattles Flock." *New York Times,* July 30, 2006.

Herberg, Will. *Protestant, Catholic, Jew: An Essay in American Religious Sociology.* Chicago: University of Chicago Press, 1983.

Hertzberg, Arthur. *The Zionist Idea: A Historical Analysis and Reader.* New York: Doubleday, 1959.

Herzl, Theodor. *The Jewish State.* 1896.

Jones, John Bush. *On Musicals, Ourselves: A Social History of the American Musical Theater.* Waltham, MA: Brandeis University Press, 2003.

Jung, C. G. *Memories, Dreams, Reflections.* New York: Pantheon Books, 1973.

———. *Psychology and Western Religion.* London: Ark Paperbacks, 1988.

Kohler, Kaufmann. *Jewish Theology: Systematically and Historically Considered.* Whitefish, MT: Kessinger Pubishing, 2007.

Kushner, Harold S. *When Bad Things Happen to Good People.* New York: Avon Books, 1983.

Lamm, Norman. *The Religious Thought of Hasidism.* New York: The Michael Scharf Publication Trust of Yeshiva University Press, 1999.

Landman, Isaac, ed. *The Universal Jewish Encyclopedia.* New York: Universal Jewish Encyclopedia, 1942.

Laqueur, Walter. *A History of Zionism: From the French Revolution to the Establishment of the State of Israel.* New York: Holt, Rinehart and Winston, 1972.

Lauterbach, Jacob Z. "Jew and Non-Jew." *CCAR Yearbook* (1921).

Levenson, Jon D. *The Death and Resurrection of the Beloved Son: The Transformation of Child Sacrifice in Judaism and Christianity.* Binghamton, NY: Vail-Ballou Press, 1993.

Levine, Amy-Jill. *The Misunderstood Jew: The Church and the Scandal of the Jewish Jesus.* San Francisco: HarperCollins, 2006.

Lilla, Mark. "The Politics of God." *New York Times Magazine,* August 19, 2007.

Lilla, Mark. *The Stillborn God: Religion, Politics, and the Modern West.* New York: Knopf, 2007.

Lindsey, Hal. *The Final Battle.* Western Front Ltd., 1995.

McFadyen, Alistair. *Bound to Sin: Abuse, Holocaust and the Christian Doctrine of Sin.* Cambridge: Cambridge University Press, 2000.

Mead, Walter Russell. "God's Country?" *Foreign Affairs,* September/October 2006.

Meyer, Michael A. *Jewish Identity in the Modern World*. Seattle: University of Washington Press, 1990.

Neusner, Jacob, William Scott Green, and Ernest S. Frerichs, eds. *Judaisms and Their Messiahs at the Turn of the Christian Era*. New York: Cambridge University Press, 1987.

Peters, F. E. *The Voice, the Word, the Books: The Sacred Scripture of the Jews, Christians, and Muslims*. Princeton, NJ: Princeton University Press, 2007.

Phillips, Kevin. *American Theocracy: The Peril and Politics of Radical Religion, Oil, and Borrowed Money in the 21st Century*. New York: Viking Penguin, 2006.

Ruether, Rosemary Radford. *Goddesses and the Divine Feminine: A Western Religious History*. Berkeley and Los Angeles: University of California Press, 2005.

Silver, Abba Hillel. *Where Judaism Differed: An Inquiry into the Distinctiveness of Judaism*. Philadelphia: Jewish Publication Society, 1957.

Stern, Chaim, ed. *Gates of Repentance*. New York: Central Conference of American Rabbis, 1978.

Stringfellow, Thornton. *A Brief Examination of Scripture Testimony on the Institution of Slavery* (1841) in *The Ideology of Slavery: Proslavery Thought in the Antebellum South, 1830–1860*, ed. Drew Gilpin Faust. Baton Rouge: Louisiana State University Press, 1981.

Talbert, Charles H. *Reading Acts: A Literary and Theological Commentary on the Acts of the Apostles*. Macon, GA: Smyth & Helwys, 2004.

Thumma, Scott. "Exploring the Megachurch Phenomena: Their characteristics and cultural context." Hartford Institute for Religion Research. http://hirr.hartsem.edu/bookshelf/thumma_article2.html.

Thumma, Scott, Dave Travis, and Warren Bird. "Megachurches Today 2005." Hartford Institute for Religion Research. http://hirr.hartsem.edu/megachurch/megastoday2005_summaryreport.html.

Tillich, Paul. *Dynamics of Faith.* New York: Harper & Row, 1957.

Weld, Theodore Dwight. *The Bible Against Slavery.* 1837.

Wright, Robert. "An Easter Sermon." *New York Times,* April 7, 2007.

Congregation Resources

The Art of Public Prayer, 2nd Edition: Not for Clergy Only *By Lawrence A. Hoffman*
6 x 9, 272 pp, Quality PB, 978-1-893361-06-5 **$19.99** *(A SkyLight Paths book)*

Becoming a Congregation of Learners: Learning as a Key to Revitalizing
Congregational Life *By Isa Aron, PhD; Foreword by Rabbi Lawrence A. Hoffman*
6 x 9, 304 pp, Quality PB, 978-1-58023-089-6 **$19.95**

Finding a Spiritual Home: How a New Generation of Jews Can Transform the
American Synagogue *By Rabbi Sidney Schwarz*
6 x 9, 352 pp, Quality PB, 978-1-58023-185-5 **$19.95**

Jewish Pastoral Care, 2nd Edition: A Practical Handbook from Traditional &
Contemporary Sources *Edited by Rabbi Dayle A. Friedman*
6 x 9, 528 pp, HC, 978-1-58023-221-0 **$40.00**

Jewish Spiritual Direction: An Innovative Guide from Traditional and Contemporary
Sources *Edited by Rabbi Howard A. Addison and Barbara Eve Breitman*
6 x 9, 368 pp, HC, 978-1-58023-230-2 **$30.00**

The Self-Renewing Congregation: Organizational Strategies for Revitalizing
Congregational Life *By Isa Aron, PhD; Foreword by Dr. Ron Wolfson*
6 x 9, 304 pp, Quality PB, 978-1-58023-166-4 **$19.95**

Spiritual Community: The Power to Restore Hope, Commitment and Joy
By Rabbi David A. Teutsch, PhD 5½ x 8½, 144 pp, HC, 978-1-58023-270-8 **$19.99**

The Spirituality of Welcoming: How to Transform Your Congregation into a
Sacred Community *By Dr. Ron Wolfson* 6 x 9, 224 pp, Quality PB, 978-1-58023-244-9 **$19.99**

Rethinking Synagogues: A New Vocabulary for Congregational Life
By Rabbi Lawrence A. Hoffman 6 x 9, 240 pp, Quality PB, 978-1-58023-248-7 **$19.99**

Children's Books

What You Will See Inside a Synagogue
By Rabbi Lawrence A. Hoffman and Dr. Ron Wolfson; Full-color photos by Bill Aron
A colorful, fun-to-read introduction that explains the ways and whys of Jewish
worship and religious life.
8½ x 10½, 32 pp, Full-color photos, HC, 978-1-59473-012-2 **$17.99**
For ages 6 & up (A SkyLight Paths book)

The Kids' Fun Book of Jewish Time
By Emily Sper 9 x 7½, 24 pp, Full-color illus., HC, 978-1-58023-311-8 **$16.99**

In God's Hands
By Lawrence Kushner and Gary Schmidt 9 x 12, 32 pp, HC, 978-1-58023-224-1 **$16.99**

Because Nothing Looks Like God
By Lawrence and Karen Kushner
Introduces children to the possibilities of spiritual life.
11 x 8½, 32 pp, Full-color illus., HC, 978-1-58023-092-6 **$17.99** *For ages 4 & up*

What Makes Someone a Jew?
By Lauren Seidman
Reflects the changing face of American Judaism.
10 x 8½, 32 pp, Full-color photos, Quality PB Original, 978-1-58023-321-7 **$8.99**
For ages 3–6

Spirituality

Journeys to a Jewish Life: Inspiring Stories from the Spiritual Journeys of American Jews *By Paula Amann*
Examines the soul treks of Jews lost and found. 6 x 9, 208 pp, HC, 978-1-58023-317-0 **$19.99**

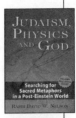

The Adventures of Rabbi Harvey: A Graphic Novel of Jewish Wisdom and Wit in the Wild West *By Steve Sheinkin*
Jewish and American folktales combine in this witty and original graphic novel collection. Creatively retold and set on the western frontier of the 1870s.
6 x 9, 144 pp, Full-color illus., Quality PB, 978-1-58023-310-1 **$16.99**
Also Available: **The Adventures of Rabbi Harvey Teacher's Guide**
8½ x 11, 32 pp, PB, 978-1-58023-326-2 **$8.99**

Ethics of the Sages: *Pirke Avot*—Annotated & Explained
Translation and Annotation by Rabbi Rami Shapiro
5½ x 8½, 192 pp, Quality PB, 978-1-59473-207-2 **$16.99** *(A SkyLight Paths book)*

A Book of Life: Embracing Judaism as a Spiritual Practice
By Michael Strassfeld 6 x 9, 528 pp, Quality PB, 978-1-58023-247-0 **$19.99**

Meaning and Mitzvah: Daily Practices for Reclaiming Judaism through Prayer, God, Torah, Hebrew, Mitzvot and Peoplehood *By Rabbi Goldie Milgram*
7 x 9, 336 pp, Quality PB, 978-1-58023-256-2 **$19.99**

The Soul of the Story: Meetings with Remarkable People
By Rabbi David Zeller 6 x 9, 288 pp, HC, 978-1-58023-272-2 **$21.99**

Aleph-Bet Yoga: Embodying the Hebrew Letters for Physical and Spiritual Well-Being
By Steven A. Rapp. Foreword by Tamar Frankiel, PhD and Judy Greenfeld. Preface by Hart Lazer.
7 x 10, 128 pp, b/w photos, Quality PB, Layflat binding, 978-1-58023-162-6 **$16.95**

Does the Soul Survive? A Jewish Journey to Belief in Afterlife, Past Lives & Living with Purpose *By Rabbi Elie Kaplan Spitz; Foreword by Brian L Weiss, MD*
6 x 9, 288 pp, Quality PB, 978-1-58023-165-7 **$16.99**

First Steps to a New Jewish Spirit: Reb Zalman's Guide to Recapturing the Intimacy & Ecstasy in Your Relationship with God *By Rabbi Zalman M. Schachter-Shalomi with Donald Gropman* 6 x 9, 144 pp, Quality PB, 978-1-58023-182-4 **$16.95**

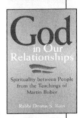

God in Our Relationships: Spirituality between People from the Teachings of Martin Buber *By Rabbi Dennis S. Ross* 5½ x 8½, 160 pp, Quality PB, 978-1-58023-147-3 **$16.95**

Judaism, Physics and God: Searching for Sacred Metaphors in a Post-Einstein World
By Rabbi David W. Nelson. 6 x 9, 368 pp, Quality PB, inc. reader's discussion guide, 978-1-58023-306-4 **$18.99**;
HC, 352 pp, 978-1-58023-252-4 **$24.99**

The Jewish Lights Spirituality Handbook: A Guide to Understanding, Exploring & Living a Spiritual Life *Edited by Stuart M. Matlins*
What exactly is "Jewish" about spirituality? How do I make it a part of my life? Fifty of today's foremost spiritual leaders share their ideas and experience with us.
6 x 9, 456 pp, Quality PB, 978-1-58023-093-3 **$19.99**

Bringing the Psalms to Life: How to Understand and Use the Book of Psalms
By Daniel F. Polish 6 x 9, 208 pp, Quality PB, 978-1-58023-157-2 **$16.95**;
HC, 978-1-58023-077-3 **$21.95**

God & the Big Bang: Discovering Harmony between Science & Spirituality
By Daniel C. Matt 6 x 9, 216 pp, Quality PB, 978-1-879045-89-7 **$16.99**

Minding the Temple of the Soul: Balancing Body, Mind, and Spirit through Traditional Jewish Prayer, Movement, and Meditation *By Tamar Frankiel, PhD, and Judy Greenfeld*
7 x 10, 184 pp, illus., Quality PB, 978-1-879045-64-4 **$16.95**
Audiotape of the Blessings and Meditations: 60 min. **$9.95**
Videotape of the Movements and Meditations: 46 min. **$20.00**

One God Clapping: The Spiritual Path of a Zen Rabbi *By Alan Lew with Sherril Jaffe*
5½ x 8½, 336 pp, Quality PB, 978-1-58023-115-2 **$16.95**

There Is No Messiah ... and You're It: The Stunning Transformation of Judaism's Most Provocative Idea *By Rabbi Robert N. Levine, DD*
6 x 9, 192 pp, Quality PB, 978-1-58023-255-5 **$16.99**

These Are the Words: A Vocabulary of Jewish Spiritual Life
By Arthur Green 6 x 9, 304 pp, Quality PB, 978-1-58023-107-7 **$18.95**

Holidays/Holy Days

Rosh Hashanah Readings: Inspiration, Information and Contemplation
Yom Kippur Readings: Inspiration, Information and Contemplation
Edited by Rabbi Dov Peretz Elkins with Section Introductions from Arthur Green's These Are the Words

An extraordinary collection of readings, prayers and insights that enable the modern worshiper to enter into the spirit of the High Holy Days in a personal and powerful way, permitting the meaning of the Jewish New Year to enter the heart.
RHR: 6 x 9, 400 pp, HC, 978-1-58023-239-5 **$24.99**
YKR: 6 x 9, 368 pp, HC, 978-1-58023-271-5 **$24.99**

Jewish Holidays: A Brief Introduction for Christians
By Rabbi Kerry M. Olitzky and Rabbi Daniel Judson
5½ x 8½, 144 pp, Quality PB, 978-1-58023-302-6 **$16.99**

Reclaiming Judaism as a Spiritual Practice: Holy Days and Shabbat
By Rabbi Goldie Milgram
7 x 9, 272 pp, Quality PB, 978-1-58023-205-0 **$19.99**

7th Heaven: Celebrating Shabbat with Rebbe Nachman of Breslov
By Moshe Mykoff with the Breslov Research Institute
5⅛ x 8¼, 224 pp, Deluxe PB w/flaps, 978-1-58023-175-6 **$18.95**

Shabbat, 2nd Edition: The Family Guide to Preparing for and Celebrating the Sabbath
By Dr. Ron Wolfson 7 x 9, 320 pp, illus., Quality PB, 978-1-58023-164-0 **$19.99**

Hanukkah, 2nd Edition: The Family Guide to Spiritual Celebration
By Dr. Ron Wolfson. Edited by Joel Lurie Grishaver.
7 x 9, 240 pp, illus., Quality PB, 978-1-58023-122-0 **$18.95**

The Jewish Family Fun Book: Holiday Projects, Everyday Activities, and Travel Ideas with Jewish Themes *By Danielle Dardashti and Roni Sarig. Illus. by Avi Katz.*
6 x 9, 288 pp, 70+ b/w illus. & diagrams, Quality PB, 978-1-58023-171-8 **$18.95**

The Jewish Lights Book of Fun Classroom Activities: Simple and Seasonal Projects for Teachers and Students *By Danielle Dardashti and Roni Sarig*
6 x 9, 240 pp, Quality PB, 978-1-58023-206-7 **$19.99**

Passover

My People's Passover Haggadah
Traditional Texts, Modern Commentaries
Edited by Rabbi Lawrence A. Hoffman, PhD, and David Arnow, PhD
A diverse and exciting collection of commentaries on the traditional Passover Haggadah—in two volumes!
Vol. 1: 7 x 10, 304 pp, HC, 978-1-58023-354-5 **$24.99**
Vol. 2: 7 x 10, 320 pp, HC, 978-1-58023-346-0 **$24.99**

Leading the Passover Journey
The Seder's Meaning Revealed, the Haggadah's Story Retold
By Rabbi Nathan Laufer
Uncovers the hidden meaning of the Seder's rituals and customs.
6 x 9, 224 pp, HC, 978-1-58023-211-1 **$24.99**

The Women's Passover Companion: Women's Reflections on the Festival of Freedom
Edited by Rabbi Sharon Cohen Anisfeld, Tara Mohr, and Catherine Spector
6 x 9, 352 pp, Quality PB, 978-1-58023-231-9 **$19.99**

The Women's Seder Sourcebook: Rituals & Readings for Use at the Passover Seder
Edited by Rabbi Sharon Cohen Anisfeld, Tara Mohr, and Catherine Spector
6 x 9, 384 pp, Quality PB, 978-1-58023-232-6 **$19.99**

Creating Lively Passover Seders: A Sourcebook of Engaging Tales, Texts & Activities
By David Arnow, PhD 7 x 9, 416 pp, Quality PB, 978-1-58023-184-8 **$24.99**

Passover, 2nd Edition: The Family Guide to Spiritual Celebration
By Dr. Ron Wolfson with Joel Lurie Grishaver 7 x 9, 352 pp, Quality PB, 978-1-58023-174-9 **$19.95**

Life Cycle
Marriage / Parenting / Family / Aging

The New Jewish Baby Album: Creating and Celebrating the Beginning of a Spiritual Life—A Jewish Lights Companion
By the Editors at Jewish Lights. Foreword by Anita Diamant. Preface by Rabbi Sandy Eisenberg Sasso.
A spiritual keepsake that will be treasured for generations. More than just a memory book, *shows you how—and why it's important*—to create a Jewish home and a Jewish life. 8 x 10, 64 pp, Deluxe Padded HC, Full-color illus., 978-1-58023-138-1 **$19.95**

The Jewish Pregnancy Book: A Resource for the Soul, Body & Mind during Pregnancy, Birth & the First Three Months
By Sandy Falk, MD, and Rabbi Daniel Judson, with Steven A. Rapp
Includes medical information, prayers and rituals for each stage of pregnancy, from a liberal Jewish perspective. 7 x 10, 208 pp, Quality PB, b/w photos, 978-1-58023-178-7 **$16.95**

Celebrating Your New Jewish Daughter: Creating Jewish Ways to Welcome Baby Girls into the Covenant—New and Traditional Ceremonies *By Debra Nussbaum Cohen; Foreword by Rabbi Sandy Eisenberg Sasso* 6 x 9, 272 pp, Quality PB, 978-1-58023-090-2 **$18.95**

The New Jewish Baby Book, 2nd Edition: Names, Ceremonies & Customs—A Guide for Today's Families *By Anita Diamant* 6 x 9, 336 pp, Quality PB, 978-1-58023-251-7 **$19.99**

Parenting As a Spiritual Journey: Deepening Ordinary and Extraordinary Events into Sacred Occasions *By Rabbi Nancy Fuchs-Kreimer* 6 x 9, 224 pp, Quality PB, 978-1-58023-016-2 **$16.95**

Parenting Jewish Teens: A Guide for the Perplexed
By Joanne Doades
Explores the questions and issues that shape the world in which today's Jewish teenagers live.
6 x 9, 200 pp, Quality PB, 978-1-58023-305-7 **$16.99**

Judaism for Two: A Spiritual Guide for Strengthening and Celebrating Your Loving Relationship *By Rabbi Nancy Fuchs-Kreimer and Rabbi Nancy H. Wiener; Foreword by Rabbi Elliot N. Dorff* Addresses the ways Jewish teachings can enhance and strengthen committed relationships. 6 x 9, 224 pp, Quality PB, 978-1-58023-254-8 **$16.99**

Embracing the Covenant: Converts to Judaism Talk About Why & How
By Rabbi Allan Berkowitz and Patti Moskovitz 6 x 9, 192 pp, Quality PB, 978-1-879045-50-7 **$16.95**

The Guide to Jewish Interfaith Family Life: An InterfaithFamily.com Handbook
Edited by Ronnie Friedland and Edmund Case 6 x 9, 384 pp, Quality PB, 978-1-58023-153-4 **$18.95**

Introducing My Faith and My Community
The Jewish Outreach Institute Guide for the Christian in a Jewish Interfaith Relationship
By Rabbi Kerry M. Olitzky 6 x 9, 176 pp, Quality PB, 978-1-58023-192-3 **$16.99**

Making a Successful Jewish Interfaith Marriage: The Jewish Outreach Institute Guide to Opportunities, Challenges and Resources *By Rabbi Kerry M. Olitzky with Joan Peterson Littman* 6 x 9, 176 pp, Quality PB, 978-1-58023-170-1 **$16.95**

The Creative Jewish Wedding Book: A Hands-On Guide to New & Old Traditions, Ceremonies & Celebrations *By Gabrielle Kaplan-Mayer* 9 x 9, 288 pp, b/w photos, Quality PB, 978-1-58023-194-7 **$19.99**

Divorce Is a Mitzvah: A Practical Guide to Finding Wholeness and Holiness When Your Marriage Dies *By Rabbi Perry Netter; Afterword by Rabbi Laura Geller.* 6 x 9, 224 pp, Quality PB, 978-1-58023-172-5 **$16.95**

A Heart of Wisdom: Making the Jewish Journey from Midlife through the Elder Years
Edited by Susan Berrin; Foreword by Harold Kushner
6 x 9, 384 pp, Quality PB, 978-1-58023-051-3 **$18.95**

So That Your Values Live On: Ethical Wills and How to Prepare Them
Edited by Jack Riemer and Nathaniel Stampfer
6 x 9, 272 pp, Quality PB, 978-1-879045-34-7 **$18.99**

About Jewish Lights

People of all faiths and backgrounds yearn for books that attract, engage, educate, and spiritually inspire.

Our principal goal is to stimulate thought and help all people learn about who the Jewish People are, where they come from, and what the future can be made to hold. While people of our diverse Jewish heritage are the primary audience, our books speak to people in the Christian world as well and will broaden their understanding of Judaism and the roots of their own faith.

We bring to you authors who are at the forefront of spiritual thought and experience. While each has something different to say, they all say it in a voice that you can hear.

Our books are designed to welcome you and then to engage, stimulate, and inspire. We judge our success not only by whether or not our books are beautiful and commercially successful, but by whether or not they make a difference in your life.

For your information and convenience, at the back of this book we have provided a list of other Jewish Lights books you might find interesting and useful. They cover all the categories of your life:

Bar/Bat Mitzvah	Life Cycle
Bible Study / Midrash	Meditation
Children's Books	Parenting
Congregation Resources	Prayer
Current Events / History	Ritual / Sacred Practice
Ecology/ Environment	Spirituality
Fiction: Mystery, Science Fiction	Theology / Philosophy
Grief / Healing	Travel
Holidays / Holy Days	12-Step
Inspiration	Women's Interest
Kabbalah / Mysticism / Enneagram	

Stuart M. Matlins, Publisher